DORLING KINDERSLEY 📖 EYEWITNESS BOOKS

ANCIENT ROME

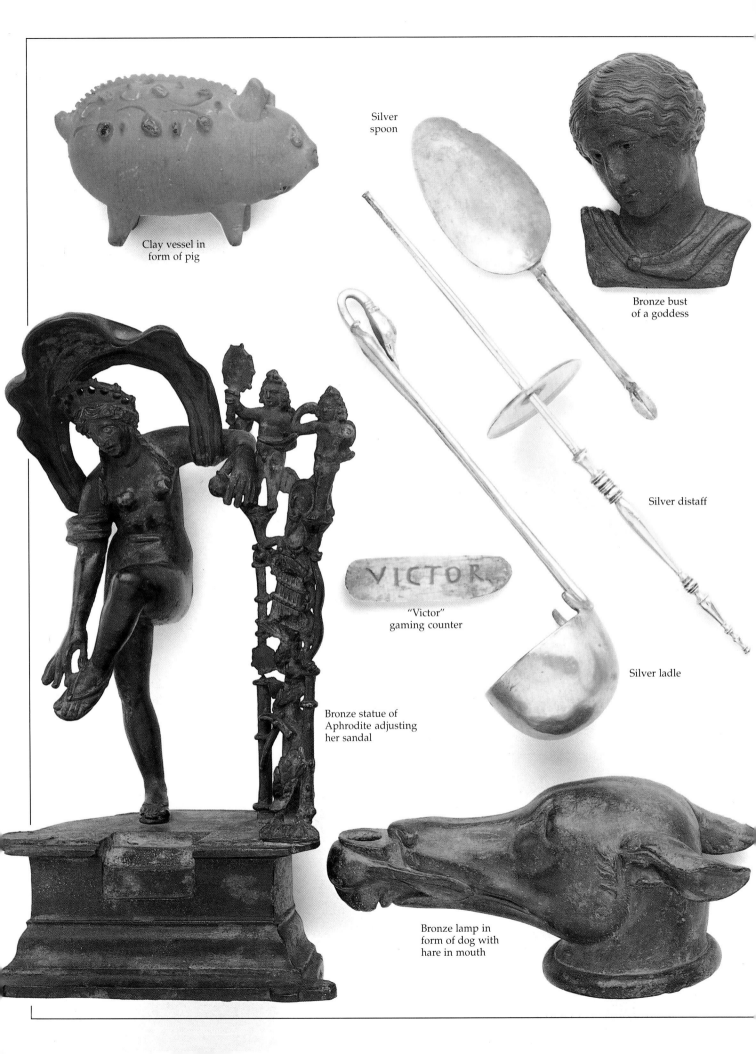

Clay vessel in
form of pig

Silver
spoon

Bronze bust
of a goddess

Silver distaff

"Victor"
gaming counter

Silver ladle

Bronze statue of
Aphrodite adjusting
her sandal

Bronze lamp in
form of dog with
hare in mouth

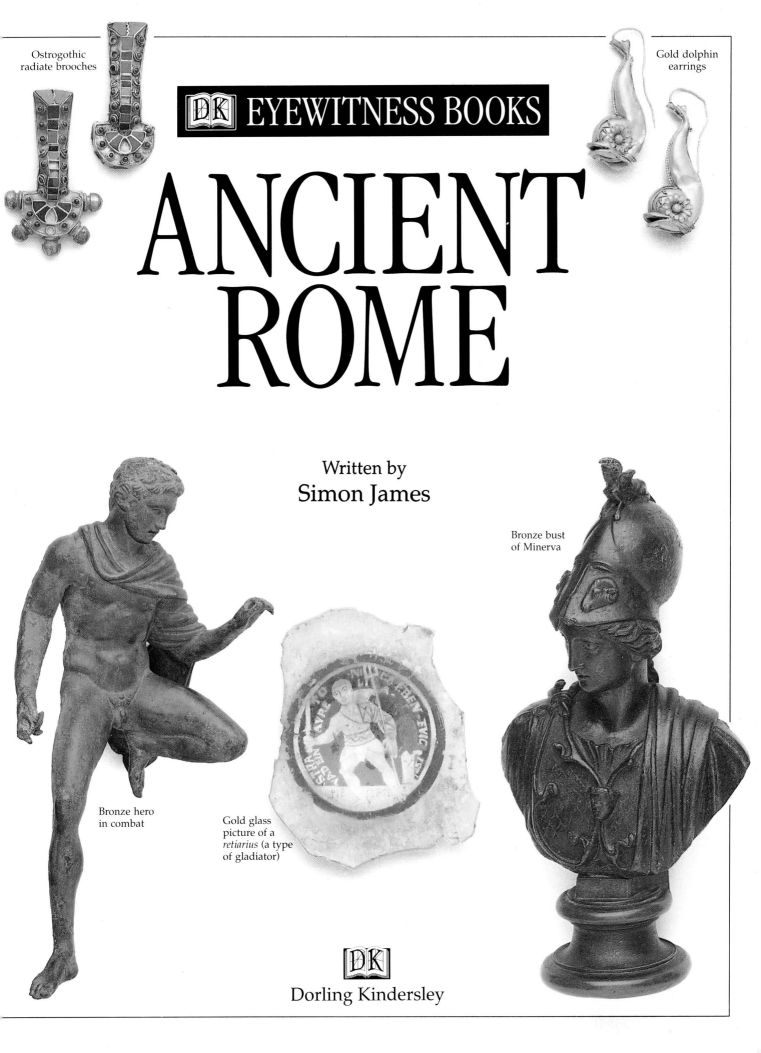

Ostrogothic
radiate brooches

Gold dolphin
earrings

DK EYEWITNESS BOOKS

ANCIENT
ROME

Written by
Simon James

Bronze bust
of Minerva

Bronze hero
in combat

Gold glass
picture of a
retiarius (a type
of gladiator)

DK

Dorling Kindersley

Bronze toilet set
for the baths

Silver brooch with
a bust of Zeus

Dorling Kindersley

LONDON, NEW YORK, AUCKLAND, DELHI,
JOHANNESBURG, MUNICH, PARIS and SYDNEY

For a full catalog, visit

DK www.dk.com

Project editor Susan McKeever
Senior art editor Julia Harris
Managing editor Sophie Mitchell
Special photography
Christi Graham and Nick Nicholls
of the British Museum
and Karl Shone

This Eyewitness ® Book has been conceived by
Dorling Kindersley Limited and Editions Gallimard

© 1990 Dorling Kindersley Limited
This edition © 2000 Dorling Kindersley Limited
First American edition, 1990

Published in the United States by
Dorling Kindersley Publishing, Inc.
95 Madison Avenue
New York, NY 10016
2 4 6 8 10 9 7 5 3

Dorling Kindersley books are available at special discounts for
bulk purchases for sales promotions or premiums. Special
editions, including personalized covers, excerpts of existing
guides, and corporate imprints can be created in large
quantities for specific needs. For more information, contact
Special Markets Dept., Dorling Kindersley Publishing, Inc.,
95 Madison Ave., New York, NY 10016; Fax: (800) 600-9098

Library of Congress Cataloging-in-Publication Data
James, Simon.
Ancient Rome / written by Simon James;
photographs by Christi Graham and Nick Nicholls.
p. cm. — (Eyewitness Books)
Summary: A photo essay documenting ancient Rome and the
people who lived there as revealed through the many artifacts
they left behind, including shields, swords, tools, toys,
cosmetics, and jewelry.
1. Rome—Antiquities—Juvenile literature. 2. Rome—Social
life and customs—Juvenile literature. [1. Rome—Antiquities.
2. Rome—Social life and customs.] I. Graham, Christi, ill.
II. Nicholls, Nick, ill. III. Title.
DG78.J36 2000 937 — dc20 90–4111
ISBN 0-7894-5789-X (pb)   ISBN 0-7894-5788-1 (hc)

Color reproduction by Colourscan, Singapore
Printed in China by Toppan Printing Co. (Shenzhen) Ltd.

Bronze boar
being led to
sacrifice

Bronze *lar*
(household god)

Contents

Clay ointment flask in form of hare

City-state to superpower

ACCORDING TO LEGEND, Rome was founded in 753 B.C. by the brothers Romulus and Remus, sons of the war god Mars. It was built on seven hills beside the Tiber River, on the border of Etruria. Early Rome was ruled by kings until 509 B.C., when the nobles drove out the wicked Etruscan king Tarquin the Proud. Rome became a republic, ruled by two consuls elected from the senate each year (p. 16). She overpowered her neighbors in Italy, and learned about Greek civilization from Greek city-states in the south. By 260 B.C. Rome had become a major force. A clash with the trading empire of Carthage in North Africa led to a century of terrible wars. Carthage was finally crushed in 146 B.C., leaving Rome as the greatest power in the Mediterranean.

ETRUSCAN DESIGN
A three-horse chariot running over a fallen man is the design for this Etruscan toilet box leg. The Etruscans may have given Rome the idea of chariot racing (p. 34) and gladiator fights in the arena (p. 30).

The Etruscans

The Etruscan people lived in northern Italian city-states and were very influenced by Greece. They were great traders, architects, and engineers, and in turn influenced early Rome, especially its religion.

REALISTIC ART
Part of a suit of armor, this shoulder guard shows a Greek grappling with one of the legendary Amazons (female warriors). The Romans admired and copied the very realistic figures of Greek art.

The Greeks

The Greeks had colonized the coasts of Sicily and southern Italy, and the fertile land had made many of the new cities wealthy, with splendid temples and richly furnished houses. These Greek colonies eventually came under Roman control, but brought with them their art, literature, and learning.

RIVER GOD
This little painted face of fired clay shows that the Greeks were skilled potters.

GODDESS OF LOVE
This silver plaque shows Aphrodite, the goddess of love. The Romans saw their goddess Venus like this.

AN ARMY OF ELEPHANTS

The growing power of Rome faced its stiffest test in 218 B.C. when the determined Carthaginian general Hannibal marched from Spain to Italy over the Alps, complete with war elephants, seen here in a 19th-century print. Hannibal smashed the legions sent against him, but Rome refused to admit defeat. He fought on in Italy for years while the Romans grimly held on, raising army after army, attacking Hannibal's bases in Spain and even landing in Africa. Finally the Carthaginians withdrew. Rome had won new lands, but the cost was terrible.

VICTORY SYMBOL

The Romans thought of the spirit of military victory as a goddess. The bronze statuette on the right shows her as an angel-like figure.

Victory statuette holds a crown of laurel leaves

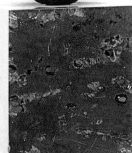

Rome expands

The clash with Carthage left Rome with her first overseas provinces, and wars with other powerful states to the east soon followed. The generals who won these conflicts brought vast wealth to Rome, but also used their soldiers to fight for personal power in Italy. Civil wars raged across the Roman world.

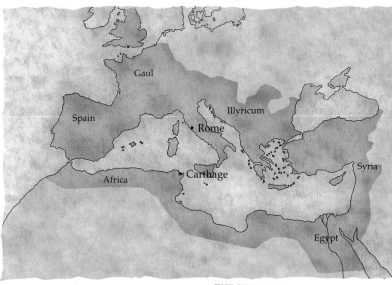

Gaul

Spain

Illyricum

Rome

Syria

Africa

Carthage

Egypt

THE SHADOW OF ROME

The Roman Empire was divided up into different provinces. Most of the Mediterranean had fallen to Rome by 50 B.C. A few more provinces were added over the next 150 years, including Britain, and the Empire was at its height by the second century A.D.

DEATH TO A DICTATOR

The most famous warring general of the late republic, Julius Caesar defeated all his rivals and eventually ruled Rome as a permanent dictator. He was too much like a king for the proud Roman senators (p. 16).

A SHIP OF WAR

The Romans learned from Carthage how to fight at sea. The clay plaque above shows a war galley, propelled by oars, with a ram at the front to sink other vessels. On the deck stand soldiers, ready to board and capture enemy ships in battle. In peacetime the fleet kept the sea lanes free of pirates.

The emperors

ROME WAS NOT ALWAYS RULED by emperors. For hundreds of years there was a republic (p. 6). But the republic collapsed in the chaos of civil wars both before and after Julius Caesar's death, when various generals fought for sole power. Order was finally restored when Julius Caesar's adopted son, Octavian (later called Augustus), was left as the only survivor of the warlords. A brilliant politician, he reformed the state and restored the Roman world to peace. He was in fact the sole ruler, with the power of the army to back him up, but he knew that Romans hated the idea of kingship. His clever solution was to proclaim the restoration of the old republic, with himself simply as first citizen. But the "new republic" was just for show; Augustus became, in fact, the first emperor, and when he died in A.D. 14, he passed the new throne to his adopted son Tiberius. Rome was to be ruled by emperors for the next 400 years.

Caligula went mad and was murdered: reigned A.D. 37-41

Claudius conquered Britain: reigned A.D. 41-54

Nero was the last of Augustus's family: reigned A.D. 54-68

HEADS AND TALES
In a world without newspapers, radio or television, coins were a good way to advertise to people the image of the emperor and his deeds. These are coins of Tiberius's successors.

A ROMAN TRIUMPH
When the emperor won a great victory, he would be granted a "triumph," the right to lead his soldiers through Rome with their prisoners and booty, while the people cheered. A slave stood behind him, holding a golden crown over his head. Captured enemy leaders would be strangled during the ceremonies.

MAD EMPEROR
Some Roman emperors went mad with power. Nero is the best known of these. Many blamed him for starting the great fire of Rome in A.D. 64, so that he could build himself a new capital on its ruins. He finally killed himself.

EMPEROR'S WEAPON
With its sword, this spectacular scabbard, decorated with gold and silver, was probably given to an officer by the emperor Tiberius himself. It was found in the Rhine River, Germany.

Tiberius receiving his nephew, the general Germanicus

THE COLOR OF POWER
Purple, the most expensive dye, was largely reserved for the emperor's clothes. Senators wore togas with a purple band. Later it became treason for anyone other than the emperor to dress completely in purple.

Murex seashells, from which purple dye was distilled

LAUREL FOR A CROWN

Roman emperors did not wear gold crowns because they did not want to be thought of as kings. But they often wore laurel wreaths to symbolize their success and military power – particularly after a conquest. Laurel leaves had long been used to make "crowns" for victorious Roman generals.

The jeweled crown was added to Augustus's head much later

CAMEO OF A GOD

A carved gem shows the first emperor, Augustus. He was thought to be very handsome, and was a patron of artists and poets. He was proclaimed a god when he died.

JULIA AND LIVIA

Members of an emperor's family were also shown in heroic poses, to promote the "royal family" image. Here Augustus's wife, Livia, is shown as the goddess Juno, and his daughter Julia as the helmeted goddess Roma. Livia and Augustus were married for 53 years and she greatly influenced him throughout his reign.

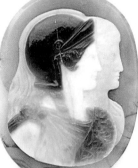

DRUSILLA

This portrait in chalcedony (a decorative stone) depicts one of the younger women in Augustus's family, probably Drusilla.

HEIR TO THE THRONE

Often the emperor adopted a promising young man as heir to the throne, to succeed him when he died. The emperor Antoninus Pius adopted Lucius Verus, who is depicted here in a fine bronze bust. Verus later became joint emperor with Marcus Aurelius, from A.D. 161-169.

A portrait of Tiberius

Traces of wood from the scabbard adhering to the steel blade

A legion's eagle standard in a shrine

The legionary

ROME OWED her great empire to her legions, perhaps the most successful armies in history. Each legion consisted of about 5,000 foot soldiers (infantry), all Roman citizens (p. 16) who joined up voluntarily for 20 to 25 years. Legionaries were rigorously trained, brutally disciplined, and well armed. They were the heart of the army and bore the brunt of battle. Their lives were hard, but they were tough. They could be mutinous – emperors made sure they treated legionaries well. In the 2nd century A.D. there were 150,000 legionaries, and even more non-citizen, auxiliary troops to aid them (p. 12). Modern replicas of legionary equipment are shown on these pages.

COMMANDING CREST
Centurions and other officers wore crests on their helmets, so that their men could see them and follow them in battle.

Crest shown in position but not attached

HEAD PROTECTOR
This helmet was cleverly designed to protect the head, face, and neck without blocking vision or hearing. It was often decorated with enameled studs.

Rome's Capitoline Hill survived capture by the Gauls in 390 B.C. because the holy geese who lived there raised the alarm and woke up the sleeping legionaries.

METAL JACKET
The famous armor of metal strips held together by leather straps on the inside was invented in the 1st century A.D. It was very flexible but heavy, and soldiers had to help each other put it on and lace it up.

UNDER THE ARMOR
A coarse woollen tunic, reaching to mid-thigh, was worn under the armor. At first the Romans did not wear trousers, but short breeches were gradually adopted.

BELTING UP
The *cingulum,* or belt, was a soldier's badge of office, worn with the tunic at all times. The "apron" of decorated leather strips gave some protection to the groin in battle. Also, the jangling noise made by the apron when the legionaries marched helped to intimidate the enemy.

The heavy pendants weighed the leather strips down

10

Specially designed point of javelin would bend when pulled out of an enemy's shield

Woollen cloak

Leather bottle for water or wine

Pack for personal items and three days' rations

PIERCING POINTS
The thrusting spear of earlier times (left) was replaced by the fearsome heavy javelin, or _pilum_ (right), which had a narrow point to pierce both shields and armor. A shower of these flying through the air would break the enemy's charge.

MARIUS'S MULE
A fully loaded legionary on the march carried more than armor, weapons, and a shield. Each man had a heavy pack held over the shoulder, which included a tool kit and a dish and pan. This burden weighed 90 lb (40 kg) or more, and often had to be carried up to 20 miles (30 km) in a day! Legionaries were called Marius's mules after the general who started the practice.

Mattock for digging ditches

Turf cutter for building turf ramparts

The sword's grip was often of wood, although bone and ivory were also used

The dagger had a double-edged blade

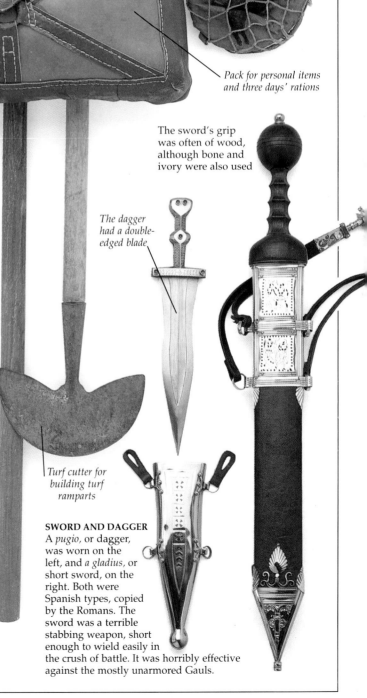

BOOTS MADE FOR WALKING
Military sandals (_caligae_) were as important as armor, because the legions won wars by fast marches as much as by battle. These boots were strong and well ventilated, with patterns of iron hobnails specially designed to take weight and withstand miles of marching.

SWORD AND DAGGER
A _pugio_, or dagger, was worn on the left, and _a gladius_, or short sword, on the right. Both were Spanish types, copied by the Romans. The sword was a terrible stabbing weapon, short enough to wield easily in the crush of battle. It was horribly effective against the mostly unarmored Gauls.

Battle and defense

By THE BEGINNING of the 1st century A.D., the Romans had acquired most of their empire; seas, deserts, mountains, and forests stopped them from going much farther. Only a few lands like Britain were added in the next hundred years. Now the soldiers were kept busy subduing uprisings and guarding the frontiers of the conquered provinces. Many of the wars at this time were fought to stop outsiders from invading the provinces. The legions remained the backbone of the army, but the auxiliary regiments (which included infantry and cavalry) became more and more important: it was their job to patrol and guard the thousands of miles of frontier that now existed around the Roman Empire.

CATAPULT BOLTS
Soldiers in the army used catapults to hurl darts and stones at the enemy. These are the iron tips from wooden darts or "bolts." Each legion had about 60 catapults, fearsome weapons used mostly in sieges.

A PROVINCE WON
Julius Caesar conquered Gaul in the 50s B.C., mainly for his own glory. Gallic resistance was finally crushed at the siege of Alesia, where Caesar trapped the Gallic leader Vercingetorix. This detail from a 19th-century painting shows the proud Gaul about to enter the Roman camp to surrender to Caesar, seated on a red platform in the distance.

AN AUXILIARY SOLDIER
Auxiliary soldiers supplemented the legions. Usually recruited from subject peoples of the empire, they were seldom citizens. This bronze statuette shows an auxiliary soldier wearing a mail shirt.

SHIELD BOSS
Roman soldiers' wooden shields had a metal cover, or boss, over the central handle. This could be used to give a hard knock to an enemy who got too close!

A ROMAN FORT
Soldiers spent the winter months, and times of peace, in timber or stone forts. On the left is the rebuilt gate of a fort at South Shields in northern England.

THE SPOILS OF WAR
An ivory plaque shows captured arms – one reward for taking over enemy territory. Plunder from conquests helped to finance the splendor of Rome, filled the emperor's coffers, and paid the troops. Rome's wars of conquest also brought several million slaves to Italy, from all over the empire.

SCALY PROTECTION
Fabric shirts covered with bronze scales were a common type of armor. Several thousand scales were stapled into rows and laced to the shirt.

The cavalry

The auxiliary cavalry were among the highest paid of Roman soldiers, partly because they had to pay for and equip their own horses. Italians were not very good horsemen, so the army raised regiments in areas where fighting on horseback was traditional, such as Gaul (ancient France), Holland, and Thrace (Bulgaria). The cavalry were the eyes of the army, patrolling and scouting ahead of the legions, guarding their flanks in battle, and pursuing defeated enemies.

A PARADE
A relief from Rome shows legionaries and galloping cavalrymen. Some of the cavalry carry standards, which were emblems of identification. The legionaries sport crests on top of their helmets (p. 10).

HARNESS FITTING
This is one of a set of fine silvered harness fittings from Xanten in Germany. Such showy equipment probably belonged to a cavalry officer.

CAVALRY SPUR
Riders used spurs attached to their shoes to urge their horses on. The stirrup had not yet been invented. Instead saddles had tall pommels, which gave riders a secure seat.

BATTLE WITH BARBARIANS
This wild entanglement of limbs, horses, and armor is a relief from a stone coffin showing Roman cavalry in combat with northern barbarians. Although the artist did not depict the soldiers very accurately, he gives a fine impression of the bloody chaos of battle.

SPEARHEADS
Auxiliary foot soldiers and horsemen used light javelins for throwing (p. 11), but heavier spears for thrusting at close range. Today only the iron spearheads survive; the wooden shafts rotted long ago. These examples come from Hod Hill in Dorset, England.

CHAMPING AT THE BIT
The Roman horse harness was basically the same as today. Leather reins and a bridle were linked to a bit which went into the horse's mouth. This one from Hod Hill is identical in form to modern snaffle bits.

Soldiers in society

Peacetime or wartime, the army played a most important role in Roman society. Many poorer people chose a career in the army because it offered a good standard of living and the chance to learn various trades such as building. There were penalties; soldiers risked death in battle, and they were not supposed to marry. But there were many benefits, and most soldiers were able to have "unofficial" wives and children. People from the provinces were rewarded for their service with Roman citizenship for them and their families. Retired legionaries were given grants of land or money. Talent could lead to promotion to centurion, in charge of a "century" of 80 men. Well-paid soldiers also provided a ready market for local traders. Settlements developed next to forts, and many grew into cities, such as York, England. Soldiers intermarrying with local women helped to spread Roman ways and weld the Empire together. The army kept the famous Roman Peace (p. 60) which brought prosperity to the provinces.

PARADE MASK
In peacetime Roman soldiers spent a lot of time training. Cavalrymen often wore elaborate armor for parades and display. This bronze mask found at Nola in Italy is from a helmet probably made specially for mock cavalry battles in which riders could practice their skills and show off their prowess.

ROOF PLAQUE
Soldiers were trained in many crafts, including building. They quarried or made their own materials, like this clay plaque for a roof. It shows the name and emblem of the 20th legion – a charging boar.

HADRIAN'S WALL
At the Emperor Hadrian's command, the army built a defensive wall in Britain to keep out the unconquered Caledonians of Scotland. Legionaries, with their technical know-how, built the wall, and the auxiliaries guarded it. Auxiliaries patrolled from forts along the wall, and the legions moved in whenever there was serious trouble. The wall ran for 75 miles (120 km).

A fanciful view of a legionary, complete with shield and spear

Elaborate hairstyle on mask

A SOLDIER'S DAUGHTER
This broken tombstone from Lancashire, England, is that of the daughter of a standard bearer. Marriages between soldiers and local women helped strengthen the empire.

PROOF OF CITIZENSHIP
When provincials serving with the auxiliaries completed 25 years of service, they were usually granted Roman citizenship, which gave important legal rights and privileges. To be able to prove their new status some soldiers had bronze copies of the official document made, like this one from Malpas, Cheshire, in England. It belonged to a Spaniard called Reburrus.

The emperor's image and titles

The lid is on the inside

MONEY PURSE
Soldiers carried cash in leather or bronze purses like this. Worn like a bracelet, the purse could be opened only when it was taken off, so it was hard to steal.

FORGOTTEN HOARD
These gold pieces, over four years' pay for a legionary, were buried in Kent, England, just after the Romans invaded Britain. They may be the savings of an officer who was killed in the fighting and so never came back for them.

Senators, citizens, subjects, and slaves

ROMAN SOCIETY had a very definite social scale. The people of the early empire were divided into Roman citizens, non-citizen provincials, and slaves. Citizens themselves were divided into different ranks, and had privileges that were denied to non-citizens. The senate in Rome, the heart of government since the Republic, was controlled by the emperor. Consuls, other magistrates, and provincial governors were chosen from its members – all wealthy men. The next rank of citizens, the equestrians, were also rich men who served in the army and administration. It was quite possible to change rank in Roman society: equestrians could become senators, and many Roman citizens had slave ancestors. Although some slaves were downtrodden, others were well treated and even powerful; for a long time the emperor's slaves and freedmen (ex-slaves) ran the civil service.

SPQR
These famous letters stand for *senatus populusque Romanus*, which means "the senate and the people of Rome." SPQR can be found on many inscriptions and coins.

BROOCH
The brooch, or *fibula*, was a common item of dress. It was handy for fastening cloaks and other garments at the shoulder.

Sprung safety pin was behind decorative front of brooch

RINGS
Rings were worn by men and women. Gold rings were a badge of rank for equestrians, and rings with carved stones were used to seal documents. Others were magic charms to ward off bad luck.

Gold signet ring

Silver rings with busts of Hercules (left) and Mars (below)

Ring made out of a gold coin

SYMBOL OF POWER
Important Roman officials were escorted by *lictors*, men who carried the *fasces* – an axe in a bundle of rods. This symbolized their authority to punish or execute people. The bronze figurine on the right dates to about the first century A.D.

Wooden rods were tied together with a strap

Axe

Nobleman

Sacrificial assistant

Priest

Priest sacrificing

MEN'S GEAR
Roman men wore a knee-length sleeveless tunic, perhaps with undergarments and various types of cloak. On formal occasions citizens wore the heavy white toga. Trousers were regarded as an unmanly foreign fashion!

Peasant

Citizen in toga

Senator

HEADED PAPER
The back of this wooden writing tablet bears the brand of the procurator of the province of Britain. It was the "headed notepaper" of the official of equestrian rank who collected taxes and paid the army in Britain. The procurator was of a lower rank than the provincial governor, a senator who commanded the army and administered justice. Both officials were selected by the emperor, and had staffs of slaves and military clerks.

On the front side there was a layer of wax to write on (p. 40)

ESCAPE FROM THE ARENA
People were made slaves in various ways: by war, by the courts, and by being born to slave parents. Most gladiators were slaves, but success in the arena could win them their freedom. Above is the bone discharge ticket to freedom of a gladiator named Moderatus.

THE FORUM
Each Roman town had a forum – a market square with public buildings around it. The forum in Rome (above) was the heart of the capital, through which ran the Sacred Way to the Capitoline Hill and the temple of Jupiter. On the right of the picture is the *curia*, or senate house. Nearby were the imperial palace and the Colosseum.

CHANGING FASHIONS
Roman men were keen followers of fashion, especially hairstyles. The Roman gentleman shown in the bronze bust sports the thick hair and clipped beard fashionable around A.D. 130. Subsequently beards were allowed to grow longer and longer, until about A.D. 230, when stubbly beards and military crewcuts came into fashion.

Clipped beard fashionable around A.D. 130

The women of Rome

W OMEN IN ROME were expected to run the household (p. 22) and be dignified wives and good mothers. Girls received very little schooling, if any at all (p. 20). The degree of freedom a woman enjoyed had a lot to do with her wealth and status. Wealthy women, especially single women and widows who controlled their own property, had a good deal of independence. Wives of emperors and senators often had a lot of influence behind the scenes. At the other end of the scale, large numbers of women were slaves, ranging from ladies' maids to farm workers.

BUST OF A WOMAN
Above is a small silver bust probably from the center of a decorative dish. It may be a portrait of a great Roman lady.

Silver distaff, used to hold wool or linen fibers being spun into thread

Bone needle

Bronze needle for finer work

Modern-looking bronze thimble

Spinning and weaving

Most Roman clothing was made of wool or linen, and the jobs of spinning and weaving yarn and making clothes were traditional wifely tasks which wealthy women avoided. The emperor Augustus made his daughter Julia do them as an example to others to keep up the old Roman ways and to demonstrate wifely virtues. Julia hated it!

Cosmetics

Many Roman women used makeup. A pale complexion was fashionable, and it was achieved by applying powdered chalk or white lead. Red ocher was used for cheek and lip color, and eyes were made up with compounds based on ash or antimony. Some cosmetics were poisonous.

Silver spatula for mixing and applying cosmetics

WOMEN'S DRESS
Roman women wore an inner and an outer tunic of wool or linen, and sometimes a cloak. The wealthy wore lightweight imported fabrics like Chinese silk and Indian cotton.

Scent bottle carved from precious onyx

This wall painting shows a girl pouring perfume into a phial

Above is an ivory comb from a grave. It is inscribed "Modestina, farewell." The poor used wooden or bone combs – more to get rid of lice than to style their hair!

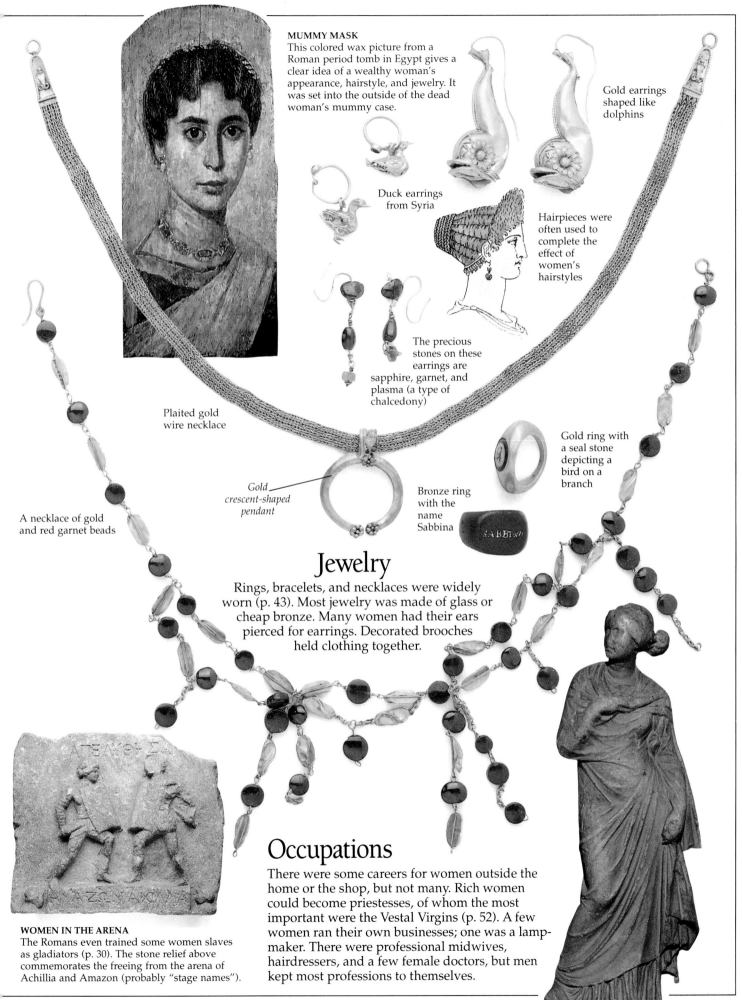

MUMMY MASK
This colored wax picture from a Roman period tomb in Egypt gives a clear idea of a wealthy woman's appearance, hairstyle, and jewelry. It was set into the outside of the dead woman's mummy case.

Gold earrings shaped like dolphins

Duck earrings from Syria

Hairpieces were often used to complete the effect of women's hairstyles

The precious stones on these earrings are sapphire, garnet, and plasma (a type of chalcedony)

Plaited gold wire necklace

Gold crescent-shaped pendant

Gold ring with a seal stone depicting a bird on a branch

Bronze ring with the name Sabbina

A necklace of gold and red garnet beads

Jewelry

Rings, bracelets, and necklaces were widely worn (p. 43). Most jewelry was made of glass or cheap bronze. Many women had their ears pierced for earrings. Decorated brooches held clothing together.

Occupations

There were some careers for women outside the home or the shop, but not many. Rich women could become priestesses, of whom the most important were the Vestal Virgins (p. 52). A few women ran their own businesses; one was a lamp-maker. There were professional midwives, hairdressers, and a few female doctors, but men kept most professions to themselves.

WOMEN IN THE ARENA
The Romans even trained some women slaves as gladiators (p. 30). The stone relief above commemorates the freeing from the arena of Achillia and Amazon (probably "stage names").

Growing up

"IS IT NEARLY OVER?"
Roman children dressed up just like their parents, and often accompanied them to official ceremonies. This detail from the Ara Pacis, a peace monument built by Augustus, shows members of the imperial family in a sacrificial procession. The children look rather unimpressed by the whole occasion!

FOR SOME LUCKY ROMAN CHILDREN, growing up consisted only of play and school. Roman fathers educated their own children until the time of the emperors, when those who could afford it hired tutors. Many also sent their children to school from the age of seven to learn the basics, with abacus and wax tablet. On the way to school children stopped at a breakfast bar (p. 44), as Italian children still do. School ran from dawn until noon; there was much learning by heart, and children were often thrashed when they made mistakes. Girls rarely received more than a basic education, after which they had to learn household skills from their mothers. Sons of the nobility would go on to prepare for a career in law or government. However, school was for the privileged few. Most children came from poor families; they could not read or write and were put to work at an early age.

YOUNG BOY
This realistic marble portrait bust depicts a young boy about five years old. The strange hair curl identifies him as a worshiper of Isis (p. 50).

Hair curl

SLEEPY SLAVE
Many Roman children were slaves. The oil flask (left) depicts a slave boy sitting on a box and dozing while he waits for his master to return. Many slaves were ill-treated and worked very long hours, so he may be taking a nap while he can. Perhaps his master is relaxing at the baths; this oil flask was probably used in bathing (p. 38).

LITTLE BOY'S LIFE
A marble relief from a sarcophagus shows scenes from the upbringing of a boy. On the left, the new-born infant is suckled by his mother and then is picked up by his father. Next the boy is shown with a donkey chariot. Finally he is seen reciting to his father.

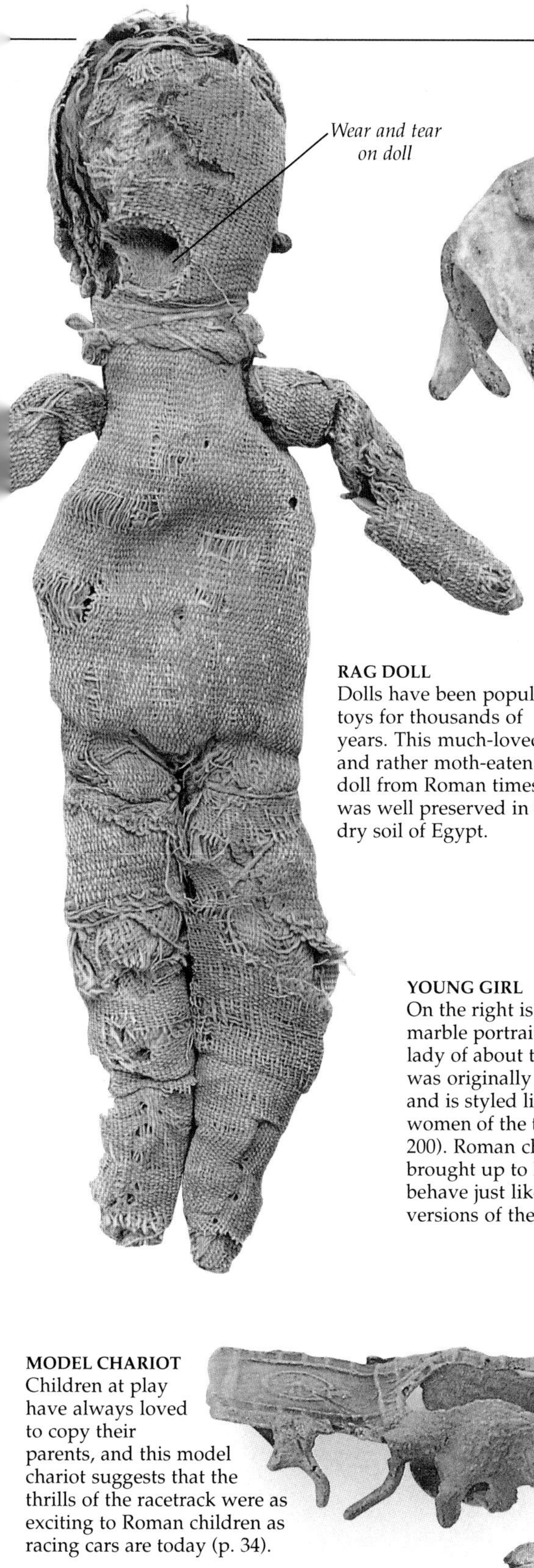

Wear and tear on doll

TOXIC TOY
Children's toys reflected the world around them, like this camel from Egypt. Its sale would be forbidden today – it is made of poisonous lead.

Glass marbles

ENDURING MARBLES
The game of marbles has remained popular through the centuries. In Roman times marbles were made of a variety of materials.

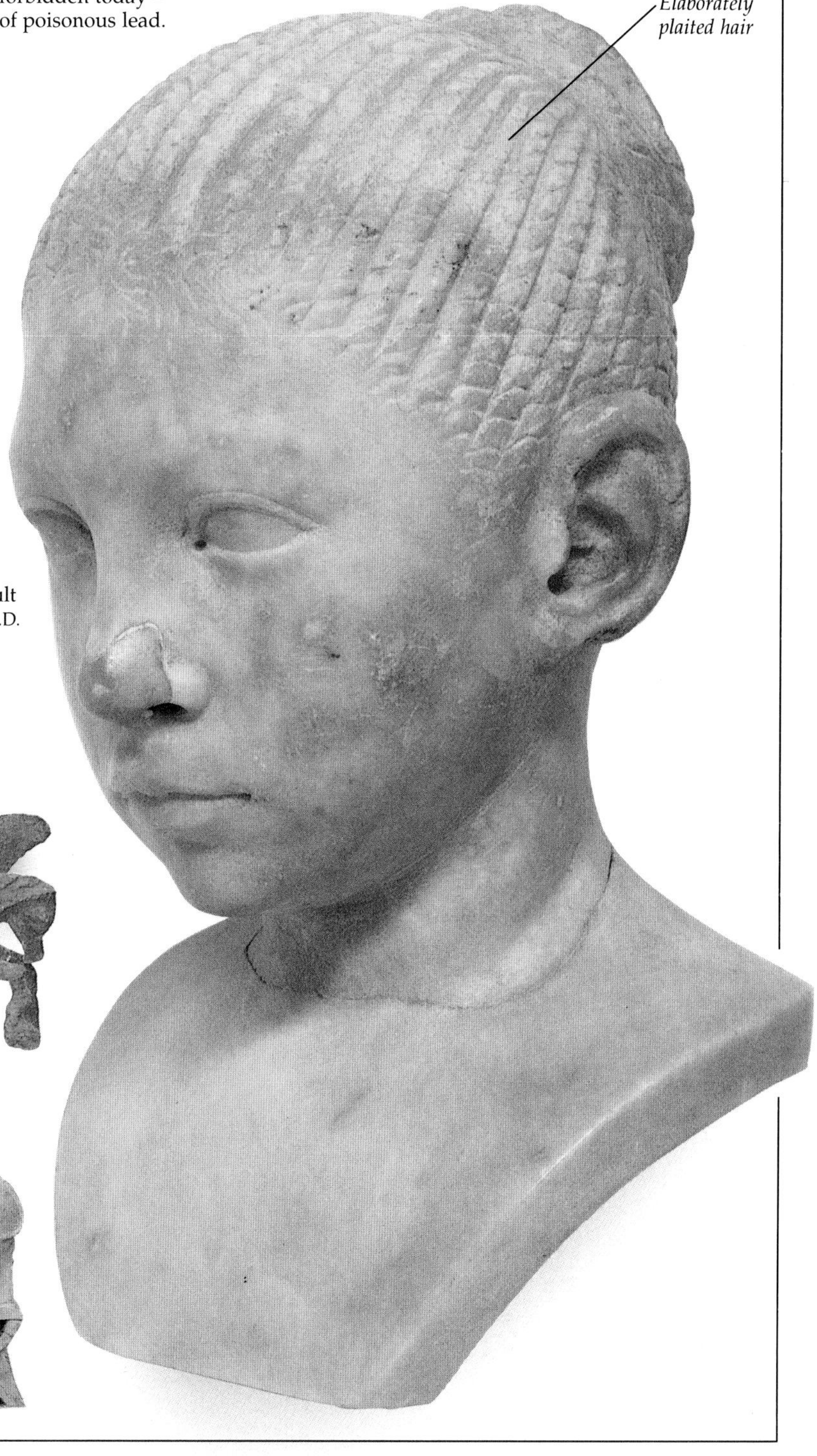

Pottery marbles

Elaborately plaited hair

RAG DOLL
Dolls have been popular toys for thousands of years. This much-loved and rather moth-eaten rag doll from Roman times was well preserved in the dry soil of Egypt.

YOUNG GIRL
On the right is a fine marble portrait of a young lady of about ten. Her hair was originally colored red, and is styled like that of adult women of the time (about A.D. 200). Roman children were brought up to look and behave just like miniature versions of their parents.

MODEL CHARIOT
Children at play have always loved to copy their parents, and this model chariot suggests that the thrills of the racetrack were as exciting to Roman children as racing cars are today (p. 34).

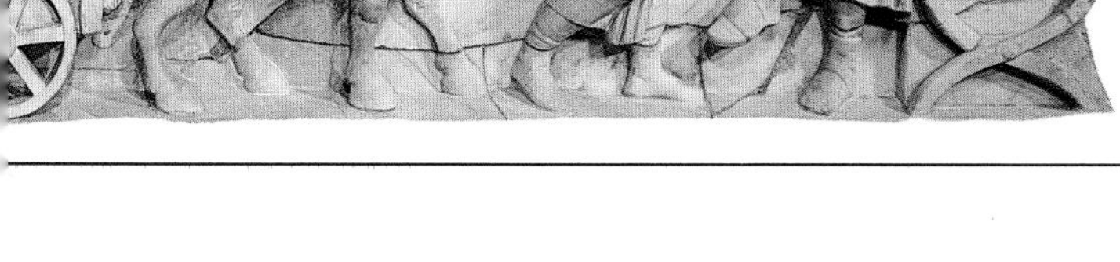

Family life

THE IDEA OF THE FAMILY was very important to the Romans, but they had a somewhat different understanding of the word than we do today. The paterfamilias, the father and head of the family, was traditionally all-powerful over the contents of his house – including all the people who lived in it, from wife to slave. He had, in theory, the power of life and death over his children. In practice, however, wives and children were not usually as downtrodden as this implies. His wife actually had her share of power, controlling the running of the house and its finances, and supervising the upbringing of the children until they were old enough to begin their schooling (p. 20). Larger households also had a number of slaves. Some were harshly treated, but others were some-times treated as members of the family.

A Roman wedding

In Roman times marriages took place often for financial or political reasons. On the wedding day the groom arrived with his family and friends at the bride's house, and the marriage took place in the atrium (p. 24) or at a nearby shrine. A sacrifice was offered, and the omens were read to make sure the gods approved. The bride and groom exchanged vows and clasped hands and so were married.

ENGAGEMENT RINGS
The groom often gave his future bride a ring with clasped hands, symbolizing marriage.

UNHAPPY FAMILY
This family portrait shows the emperor Septimus Severus with his wife and sons Caracalla and Geta. This imperial family was not a happy one; after Severus died, Caracalla murdered Geta before being killed himself. After this, his memory was officially cursed, and his portrait (above left) was defaced.

Slaves and pets

To modern eyes, wealthy Roman households would have seemed crowded and lacking in privacy, with slaves scurrying around cleaning, carrying things, and tending to the needs of the family. The household also included working animals: guard dogs, hunting dogs on country estates, perhaps horses, and cats to chase rats. There were also lap dogs, caged birds, and other pets, mainly for the children.

FREED SLAVE
Hedone, freed maidservant of Marcus Crassus, set up this bronze plaque to the goddess Feronia, who was popular with freed slaves.

SAD SLAVE?
Above right is a model of a kitchen slave weeping as he works at the *mortarium* (p. 44). He is either unhappy with his hard life, or grinding up a strong onion!

GUARD DOG
There were many breeds of dog in the Roman Empire, including fierce guard dogs like the one on the right, kept chained at the door to deter thieves.

Dog collar

DOG TAG
Some Roman dogs wore identity tags in case they got lost. This bronze tag from a dog says "Hold me if I run away, and return me to my master Viventius on the estate of Callistus."

Household gods

Most Romans were religious and respected their many gods (p. 50), especially the particular gods and spirits who protected each home from evil. Every house had its own shrine, where the whole family worshiped daily. It was also very important to remember the family ancestors. Senatorial families kept wax masks or portraits of their ancestors, and most people would regularly go to the family graves to pay homage to the dead (p. 56).

Crest on snake's head

LAR
The *lar* was a spirit of the family's ancestors. The bronze *lar* on the left, who is pouring wine from a drinking horn in one hand while holding a libation bowl in the other, is making a sacrifice (p. 52).

Libation bowl was used to pour liquids onto the sacrificial fire on the altar

SNAKE SPIRIT
The dwelling place had its own protective spirit, which was depicted as a bearded snake (see the shrine below).

A ball of incense about to be burned on an altar

GENIUS
The *genius* was the personal protective spirit of a man (a woman was guarded by a Juno; p. 50). This *genius* wears a toga over his head in the pose of a priest sacrificing.

HOUSEHOLD SHRINE
The *lararium*, or household shrine, from a Pompeii house (left), is shaped like a little temple. A *genius* stands in the middle, flanked by two *lars*, and a snake below.

DEDICATED EX-SLAVES
Romans often had very good relations with their slaves, and when they freed them became their patrons. This marble tomb monument shows Lucius Antistius Sarculo and his wife, Antistia, framed by shells, an indication that they have died. The inscription records that it was set up by Rufus and Anthus, two of their freedmen, to their deserving patrons. Clearly Rufus and Anthus greatly admired their former masters, and must have become wealthy themselves to be able to afford such a splendid monument. Even more interestingly, Antistia had once been a slave herself; Antistius had freed her, then married her.

House and home

IF YOU WERE A WEALTHY ROMAN, you could afford to have both a town house and a country villa (p. 58). Wealthy Romans' homes were usually of the same basic design. The front door opened into an atrium, or hall, which had an opening to the sky and a pool in the middle of the floor. A peristyle, or colonnaded garden, at the back added to the airy feeling of the house – needed in the fierce heat of the Italian summer. The rooms were uncluttered and elegant, with high ceilings and wide doors but few windows. Although the walls were brightly painted and the floors were often richly decorated with mosaics, there was surprisingly little furniture: strongboxes, beds, couches mainly for dining, small tables, and perhaps some fine wooden cupboards. But only the lucky few enjoyed the luxury of such a fine house. The great mass of the people lived in rural poverty or in tall and crowded city tenements. The tenements had no sanitation and were a constant fire hazard. The ground floor was usually occupied by a row of shops.

HOUSEHOLD WILDLIFE
As in Italy today, houses and gardens had their own brand of wildlife: scorpions in dark corners and lizards basking on sunny walls.

CAT AMONG THE PIGEONS
Many mosaics captured scenes from everyday life, like this one of a cat which has just caught a pigeon. The picture is made up of several thousand tiny pieces of colored stone, each about .2 in (5 mm) square. They were laid in wet plaster by expert mosaic makers.

Lizards like this bronze model still live in the ruins of Pompeii

UNDER LOCK AND KEY
The Romans had locks and keys as a precaution against burglars. The complicated shape of the end of the key (right) fitted through a keyhole into the pattern of holes in the hidden bolt (left), allowing the bolt to be moved back and forth to lock or unlock a trunk or chest.

Pattern of holes in bolt matches key shape

Lock with special shape on end for fitting into bolt

Cogs connected to handles on the outside

A STRONGBOX
This strongbox has two sliding bolts in the lid (shown turned over). These were operated by turning the cogs from the outside. There were also two catches at the upper end, one worked by a bolt, the other by gravity; it only released itself when the box was turned on its side. These boxes would have contained money and valuables.

COUCH END
This carved ivory plaque from the side of a couch shows Cupid, the god of love, hovering above Bacchus, the god of wine, clutching a bunch of grapes. Wealthy Romans spent a lot on furnishings and table-ware to impress their guests at their sumptuous dinner parties (p. 46).

ELEPHANT LEG
This brightly colored bronze elephant's head was in fact a leg from a piece of furniture – probably a couch. It may have been modeled on one of the many elephants brought over from Africa to die in the arena (p. 32). The entertainment held in the amphitheater was a popular theme in Roman art and architecture.

The foot looks like a lion's paw

(p. 32)

LIGHTING-UP TIME
Romans lit their houses with oil lamps of pottery or bronze. The lamps could be quite elaborate, like this bronze one in the shape of a grotesque head. The lamps burned olive oil, which was quite expensive and not very bright. It was often a better idea to go to bed as soon as it got dark!

The ears make brackets for attaching the leg

Oil was poured into this hole, which was originally covered with a hinged lid

AN ATRIUM
Wealthy Romans' houses had an atrium inside the front door where guests were received. This restoration of an atrium in a Pompeii house shows the opening to the sky for light. The central pool helped to keep it cool.

Copper and silver inlay

Position of couch end on couch

MULE-HEADED
One of a pair of end supports from a couch, the cast bronze piece below is decorated with the figure of a satyr and a mule's head. The position of the couch end can be seen in the reconstruction above. Each couch held up to three people, who lay side by side.

This graceful figure, part of a wall painting from Stabiae, near Pompeii, represents spring

Builders and engineers

THE ROMANS were great builders, constructing temples, country houses, and magnificent public buildings of carved marble. Although they adopted many Greek architectural styles, they had their own trademarks. They invented the dome and made great use of arches. They used fired bricks and developed concrete by mixing *pozzolana*, a strong volcanic material, with rubble. Their structures had a long life span – even the mosaics they used in decorating are perfectly preserved in many places. Romans also had sound engineering skills; they brought water supplies to cities along aqueducts, and built roads and bridges that are in use to this day.

PONT DU GARD, FRANCE
A vast stone three-storied bridge carried an aqueduct over a gorge. The water flowed through a covered channel along the top. The aqueduct ran for about 30 miles (50 km), ending in a reservoir which supplied 22,000 tons of water to the city of Nîmes every day.

PLUMB BOB
A simple bronze weight on a string, called a plumb bob, gave a perfectly vertical line to make sure walls were straight. The owner's name, Bassus, is inscribed on the bob. Such simple tools were used to plan and build the Pont du Gard (above).

The foot-rule is divided into 12 Roman inches

BRONZE FOOT-RULE
This folding bronze rule was probably owned by a Roman stonemason or a carpenter, and was easily carried on a belt or in a bag. It is one Roman foot long (11 2/3 in; 296 mm).

The dividers are tightened with a wedge

BRONZE DIVIDERS
Proportional dividers like these were used by engineers when working with scale plans and models. The gap between the lower points is always twice that between the upper points, allowing, for example, statues to be copied at twice, or half, natural size.

BRONZE SQUARE
Used for checking the squareness of shapes, this tool would have been useful to carpenters, stonemasons, mosaic makers, and other craftsmen. It measures 90 and 45 degree angles.

A ROMAN ROAD
Roads were usually very straight, and carefully built with a camber (hump) so that rainwater drained off into ditches. This made the roads usable in all weather. Each road was made up of several levels, with a firm foundation. Gravel or stone slabs covered the surface.

CHISEL
Romans used chisels like this iron one when they worked with wood. Wood was used a lot in building, especially for roof frames, but, like this chisel's handle, most Roman wood has long since rotted.

Roman plumbing

The water supply system was very advanced in many Roman cities, more so than anything else until the 19th century. The great aqueducts supplied many water outlets, including public fountains in **the** streets (from which most people fetched their domestic water in buckets). Bathhouses had their own supply (p. 38), as did public toilets. Larger private houses often had water from a main, and also collected rainwater from the roof (see the atrium on p. 25). Elaborate systems of lead pipes fed the water to these places under gravity, and after use a system of underground sewers carried the waste away.

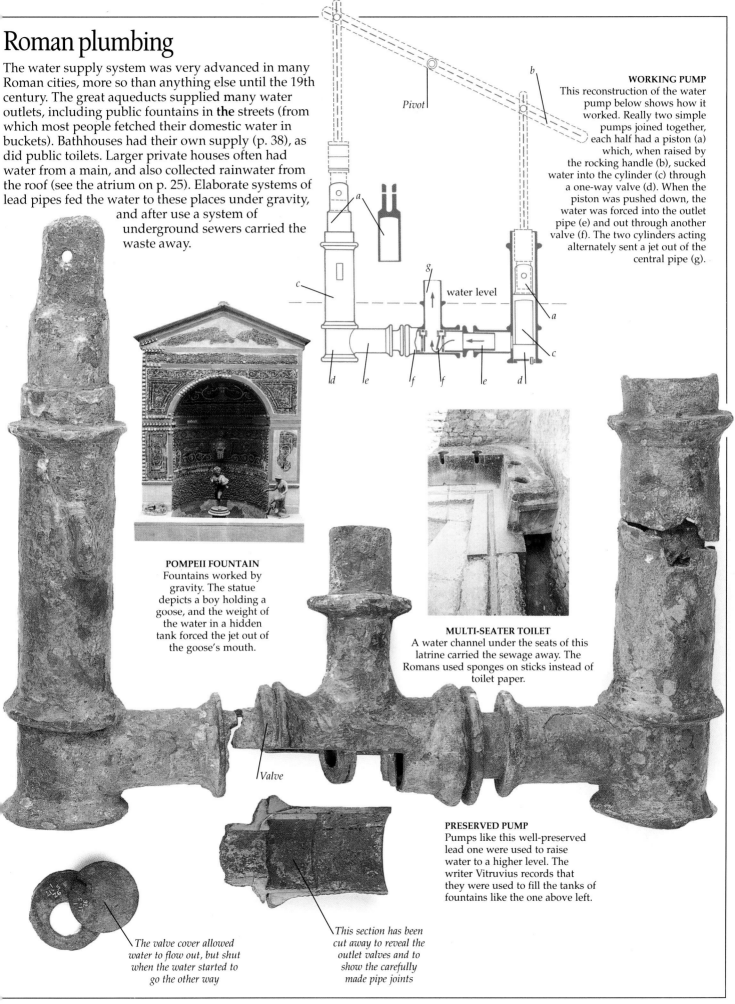

Pivot

WORKING PUMP
This reconstruction of the water pump below shows how it worked. Really two simple pumps joined together, each half had a piston (a) which, when raised by the rocking handle (b), sucked water into the cylinder (c) through a one-way valve (d). When the piston was pushed down, the water was forced into the outlet pipe (e) and out through another valve (f). The two cylinders acting alternately sent a jet out of the central pipe (g).

water level

POMPEII FOUNTAIN
Fountains worked by gravity. The statue depicts a boy holding a goose, and the weight of the water in a hidden tank forced the jet out of the goose's mouth.

MULTI-SEATER TOILET
A water channel under the seats of this latrine carried the sewage away. The Romans used sponges on sticks instead of toilet paper.

Valve

PRESERVED PUMP
Pumps like this well-preserved lead one were used to raise water to a higher level. The writer Vitruvius records that they were used to fill the tanks of fountains like the one above left.

The valve cover allowed water to flow out, but shut when the water started to go the other way

This section has been cut away to reveal the outlet valves and to show the carefully made pipe joints

27

The bloody arena

THE COLOSSEUM IN ROME is a marvel of Roman engineering and the greatest of the many amphitheaters of the empire. Opened by the emperor Titus in A.D. 80, it held about 50,000 people and was designed so well that everyone could have got out of the building in a few minutes. The secret was in the skilled use of arched vaults, and the corridors and stairways leading to the seating. The arched vaults on the ground floor formed 80 entrances for the crowds, each marked with a number to help visitors to find their seats. A huge canvas awning was often stretched over the top to provide shade from the sun, and for nighttime shows a massive iron chandelier was suspended above the arena. However, this extraordinary building was constructed for a horrible purpose: to allow people to watch killing and bloodshed for amusement. Gladiators fought each other to the death, and other men fought animals from the four corners of the Roman world. These so-called games were public shows paid for by emperors and other important Romans to gain popularity.

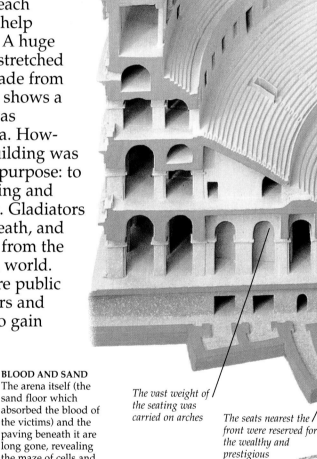

Masts for the cables which held the awning

The vast weight of the seating was carried on arches

The seats nearest the front were reserved for the wealthy and prestigious

The maze of corridors, cells, and machinery beneath the arena

BLOOD AND SAND
The arena itself (the sand floor which absorbed the blood of the victims) and the paving beneath it are long gone, revealing the maze of cells and passages below. There were hidden elevators and trap-doors to allow animals and men to appear from beneath the surface.

SEA BATTLE FOR FUN
The Roman people grew bored with mere slaughter, and emperors tried hard to find novel forms of butchery to amuse them. When it first opened, the Colosseum's arena could be filled with water, and "sea battles" were fought by gladiators in small ships, here imagined by an 18th-century artist.

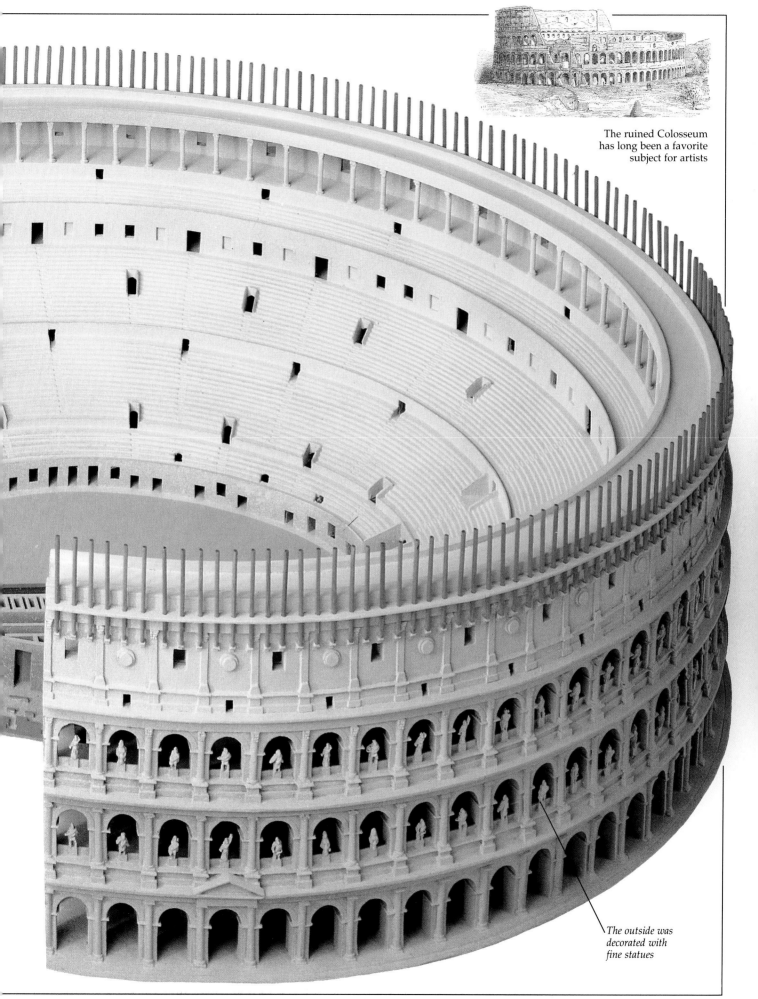

The ruined Colosseum has long been a favorite subject for artists

The outside was decorated with fine statues

Mortal combat

GLADIATOR FIGHTS WERE PROBABLY religious in origin, first held at funerals to honor the deceased. But by the time of the emperors, they had become simply a blood sport which almost everyone enjoyed; there were only a few protesting voices. Most gladiators were slaves or criminals and were trained in special schools. If they were lucky, they survived to win their freedom. Many thought the gladiator's way of life was glamorous. At Pompeii someone wrote graffiti on a wall about a Thracian called Celadus: "the man the girls sigh for." Some men ever volunteered to be gladiators, and the emperor Commodus shocked Rome by fighting in the arena himself. But for many of these trained murderers, life was brutal and short. There were various types of gladiators, each with distinct weapons. Regular spectators had their favorites: the emperor Titus liked Thracians; Claudius detested *retiarii*.

SMALL SHIELD
A small bronze shield like this might have been carried by a Thracian (p. 33). Originally it was burnished to a bright golden color. It did not offer much protection in the fight.

THE NET MAN
One type of gladiator, the nimble *retiarius* (net man), is shown in this gold glass picture. He was equipped like a fisherman with a weighted net to catch his foe, and Neptune's trident to stab him. If he lost his net the unarmored *retiarius* was usually doomed.

Decorative bronze crest

A bust of Hercules

Flap at back protected neck

Twist key

HANDSOME HELMET
An elaborate bronze helmet like this one would have been worn by one of the more heavily armed gladiators. It gave good protection to the head, but the wearer could not see very well – dangerous when fighting the speedy *retiarius*. When in action, the face guard was locked with twist keys at the front. Gladiators' armor was designed to look flashy, but it left vital areas like the stomach unprotected from deadly blows.

These large flaps protected the throat

Steel and claws

The games in the amphitheater lasted all day. In the morning wild animals were brought on to fight each other or to face "huntsmen," or simply to kill defenseless criminals. Some Christian martyrs died this way, although no definite cases are recorded of this in the Colosseum. Around midday there would be a break for the bodies to be removed and fresh sand spread while excitement rose in anticipation of the main attraction in the afternoon: the gladiators.

ELEPHANT
In their endless quest for novelty in the arena, the Romans scoured the known world for exotic animals like this African elephant.

BOUND FOR DEATH
All sorts of animals from foreign lands, like this antelope, were captured and put on ships bound for Rome and the Colosseum. It was so important to the emperors to put on lavish spectacles that they spent vast sums on this horrible trade.

Unprotected shoulder

Leopard is lunging at protected part of arm

"THE BRUTE TAMER OF POMPEII"
The Victorians were as fascinated as anyone by the horrors of the arena. This 19th-century lion tamer used "Roman" costume as a gimmick in his act.

BEAR
Bears were to be found within the empire for entertainment in the arena, and sometimes rarer animals from beyond the Roman world were obtained. These included polar bears, Indian tigers, and rhinoceroses.

SURPRISE ATTACK
A clay plaque shows a leopard springing at an unwary *bestiarius* (animal fighter). Some of the huntsmen liked to show off by fighting big cats while on stilts, but the spectators enjoyed watching the hunters die as much as they liked to see the animals being killed; it was all part of the "fun."

DEADLY DESIGNS

On the left is part of the intricate face guard of a gladiator's helmet. The holes were small enough to protect the face from sword and trident without blocking the view too much. If the wearer was killed, the valuable armor was repaired and passed on to another man.

THE FINAL MOMENT

The last tense moment of a fight is shown on this oil lamp. A wounded gladiator stares death in the face as the victor stands over him ready to deliver the final blow.

Shoulder guard to protect the neck

The gladiators

"We who are about to die salute you!" shouted the gladiators to the emperor, and the fighting began, to musical accompaniment (p. 48). Several pairs or groups fought at a time. When a gladiator was wounded he could appeal for mercy. The emperor listened to the crowd's opinion; had the gladiator fought well enough to be spared? If not, the people jabbed downward with their thumbs, and he was killed.

A LIFE IN THE BALANCE

A bronze statuette of one of the heavily armed gladiators shows his armor on head, arms, and legs, and his unprotected stomach. His shield stands on the ground. He is probably wounded and appears to be raising his left hand in an appeal to be spared.

Curved sword

LIGHTLY ARMED

Some gladiators were lightly armed, as shown in these bronze figurines. On the left is a Thracian carrying a curved dagger and a very small shield; on the right is a *retiarius* (p. 31).

SCREEN GLADIATOR

The motion picture *Spartacus* brought the terror of the arena back to life. Here, Spartacus himself, armed as a Thracian (although without a helmet), fights a *retiarius*. He has lost his shield and has grabbed his foe's net to avoid being tripped.

DUEL TO THE DEATH

A clay plaque shows two heavily armed gladiators fighting it out, one thrusting at his opponent's neck, the other going for the vulnerable abdomen.

A day at the races

ALL OVER THE ROMAN EMPIRE, people flocked to see the "races" in their spare time. A day at the races meant a day spent betting on teams, cheering, and buying snacks from vendors. In an atmosphere charged with excitement, chariots creaked and horses stamped in the starting boxes. At the drop of a white cloth, the starting signal, the gates flew open, and the horses were off in a cloud of dust, thundering around the *spina* or central barrier. The audience went wild, cheering their chosen team – in the capital, the four teams were the Blues, Greens, Reds, and Whites, owned by the emperor. People followed their favorite teams and drivers with the passion of modern sports fans everywhere. Sometimes rivalry between fans led to violence. Fighting between the Blues and the Greens in Constantinople in A.D. 532 developed into a rebellion against the government in which thousands died.

THE WINNER
A victorious charioteer (above) received a victor's palm and a purse of gold, and was hailed as a hero.

WATCHING THE SHOW
This mosaic shows people watching the races. Here, men and women could sit together, unlike at other shows. The poet Ovid records that the racetrack was a good place to meet a boyfriend or a girlfriend!

Chariots were very light for maximum speed

BEN HUR
The epic film *Ben Hur* tried to capture the excitement and danger of a charioteer's life. Controlling a *quadriga* – four horses at full gallop – was quite a task, especially on the turns, which held a special peril. At these, many charioteers took a tumble.

CHARIOT AND HORSE
Chariots called *bigae* were pulled by two horses; *quadrigae* had four horses. Special stables housed the trained racehorses. This bronze model is of a *biga*; one of the horses is missing. Races consisted of up to 12 chariots running seven laps, a total of about 5 miles (8 km). There were frequent crashes, injuries, and deaths, but they just added to the excitement of the hard-bitten racegoers. Chariots that had lost their drivers could still win a race if they crossed the line first.

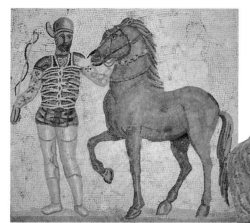

ONE MAN AND HIS HORSE
This charioteer from the Blues team wears a leather harness to protect him in a fall. Successful charioteers often became very famous. And although mostly slaves, they sometimes made enough money to buy their freedom. Their racehorses had names like Candidus (Snowy), Rapax (Greedy), and Sagitta (Arrow).

Ram's head finial on top of chariot pole

Champion stallions were used for breeding during their racing years

POLE END
This bronze finial, or chariot pole decoration, shows a figure of a triton (merman). Chariots were built for looks as well as speed and could be splendidly decorated.

The triton blows a seashell trumpet

RECONSTRUCTED RACETRACK
The greatest racetrack of all, the Circus Maximus in Rome, seated up to 250,000 people. The chariots erupted from the starting gates set up on the long straight and thundered round in an counterclockwise direction. Seven laps later, the survivors crossed the finish line opposite the imperial box, on the left.

The theater

THE ROMANS largely copied theater from Greece, and the best actors of Roman plays were usually Greek. Stage shows were first put on as part of religious festivals, and were later paid for by the wealthy to gain popularity. Tickets were free – if you could get them. Although Romans of all classes enjoyed the plays, they thought the actors were a scandalous lot. Women were not allowed to sit near the front, in case they were tempted to run off with one of the performers! In writing comedies Roman playwrights like Plautus imitated Greek play scripts. The stories were about people like kidnapped heiresses, foolish old men, and cunning slaves, and usually had a happy ending. Roman audiences preferred comedies to tragedies. The Romans also invented their own types of performance, such as mime. Another Roman form, called pantomime, involved one actor dancing and miming a story from Greek legend to an accompaniment of singing and music.

MOSAIC MASKS
Roman actors were men (women could appear only in mimes), and they wore elaborate masks, like these in a mosaic from Rome. The masks indicated the sorts of characters portrayed, both young and old, male and female, gods and heroes. They were lightweight, but hot to wear.

A COMIC ACTOR
The cheeky, scheming slave was one of the standard characters of Roman comedy. When his plans were found out, he often ended up taking refuge in a temple, sitting on the altar, like the bronze figure above. Here he was safe from his pursuers until he moved!

TRAGIC FACE
Theater masks were favorite themes in Roman art. On the left is a marble carving of a female tragic mask. Actual masks were probably made of shaped and stiffened linen. There was a gaping mouth for the actor to speak through, and holes for him to see through.

A TROUPE OF PLAYERS
A mosaic, now in Naples, Italy, shows a group of actors in costumes and masks, dancing and playing musical instruments (p. 48). The piper is dressed as a woman and is wearing the white mask of a female character.

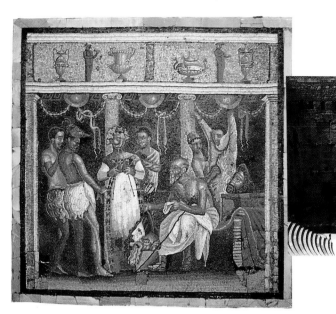

A ROMAN THEATER
Roman theaters were usually open to the sky. The one at Orange, France, could hold 9,000 people on the curving banks of seats. The massive wall at the back of the stage once had 76 decorative stone columns and many statues. It also had three doors through which the actors made their entrances.

BEHIND THE SCENES
A mosaic from Pompeii shows a group of Greek actors rehearsing a play. You can see two actors practicing dance steps, and another being helped into his costume. A musician plays the double pipes, and masks lie ready to be worn.

Dagger

Bag of money

Lamp

Unlike Roman actors, mimes did not wear masks

Figure holding a dagger

Figure holding a bag of money

The classic symbol of theater: tragic and comic masks

Figure holding a lamp

THREE MIMES
These terra-cotta figures show a group of mimes performing a play. The mime was a favorite of the ordinary townsfolk. It was a sort of crude comedy, and was very different from modern mime, because the actors spoke. It was also different from other Roman stage shows, because it was often performed on rough wooden stages set up in the streets, the actors did not wear masks, and women played female roles. Mime had regular characters, like Stupidus, the fool. You can guess the sort of plot mimes had from the objects these clay figures hold. Perhaps this one was about hidden treasure and double-crossing!

A trip to the baths

BATH HOUSE FOUNDATIONS
These foundations of a bath house were revealed in London, England, in 1989. The bottoms of the brick pillars which once supported the raised floor can be seen. Hot air circulating through this space heated the floor and the room above it (see below).

Fᴇᴡ ʀᴏᴍᴀɴ ʜᴏᴜsᴇs had their own baths; most people went to large public bathing establishments. These were not just places to get clean. Men went to the baths after a day's work to exercise, play games, meet friends, chat, and relax. Women went to their own separate baths, or used the public baths in the morning. Besides an exercise yard, or hall, there were the complicated bath buildings themselves. Changing rooms, where people left all their clothes on shelves, led to a series of progressively hotter chambers. The heat could be either dry (like a sauna) or steamy (like a Turkish bath), and the idea was to clean the pores of the skin by sweating. Soap was a foreign curiosity; olive oil was used instead. Afterward there were cold plunge-baths or swimming pools to close the pores. This might be followed by a relaxing massage, before going home for dinner (p. 46).

Ivory counters for a board game

The inscription on the above counter means "bad luck"

Ivory (above), bone (above right), and glass gaming counters

Agate dice

Rock crystal dice

Metal dice shaped like squatting men

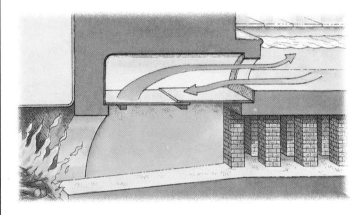

HEATING THE BATHS
Fires stoked by slaves from outside the bath building sent hot air under the floors and through hollow tiles in the walls to chimneys in the roof. The floors and walls became so hot that people inside had to wear wooden clogs to avoid burning their feet. The fires were also used to boil water in tanks and to heat pools, as the drawing on the left shows.

THE BATHS AT BATH
The natural hot spring at Bath, England was used by the Romans as the center of a medical bathing complex. Sick people came from all over the country to seek a cure by swimming in the waters and praying to Sulis, the Celtic goddess of the place, whom the Romans identified with Minerva (p. 50). People still use the waters for their health-giving properties today.

Games and gambling

People came to the baths to exercise and play in the yard, some perhaps training with weights, others playing ball games. These included catching games, which involved counting scores, and were played with colored balls of all sizes including heavy medicine balls. The less energetic bought drinks and snacks from vendors, or sat in the shade playing board games or gambling with dice (a favorite pastime of Augustus). Such games were also played in taverns and at home, away from the noise and bustle of the bath house.

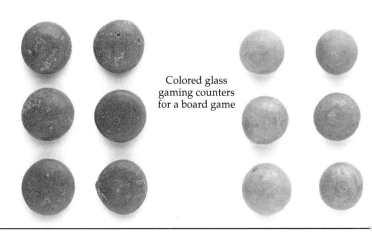

Colored glass gaming counters for a board game

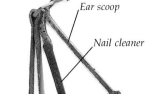

Ear scoop

Nail cleaner

Tweezers

POCKET SIZE
Dating to the 1st or 2nd century A.D., this bronze pocket toilet set from London includes useful implements for personal hygiene.

Handle from which to hang cleaning implements

Detachable lid of oil flask

SPONGES AND STRIGILS
This 19th-century watercolor (above) by Sir Lawrence Alma-Tadema depicts women cleaning themselves with sponges and strigils at the Roman baths.

Slot for hanging or attaching to a carrying handle (above right)

A COLD SPLASH
Pouring dishes, or *paterae*, like this bronze example (left) were used for splashing cold water over the body to close the pores of the skin after the heat of the baths. Many people got attendants or their own slaves to do this for them.

Base of patera *has corroded through over the centuries*

ALL SET FOR THE BATHS
This set of utensils would leave you well equipped for a visit to the baths. The oil flask and the pair of strigils (for scraping the oil, sweat, and dirt from the skin) are attached to a carrying handle. This was like a large key-ring, allowing the implements to be easily removed.

Curved part of strigil was used for scraping off dirt

OIL FLASK
Decorated with three African faces, perhaps slave bath attendants, this 2nd-century oil flask may be the earliest depiction of black people to be found in Britain.

Writing it all down

DOZENS OF TONGUES were spoken across the Roman Empire, but Latin in the west and Greek in the east were the languages spoken and written for international communication, government, and trade. The Romans introduced writing to northern Europe for the first time, and the Latin alphabet is still used there. There were only 22 letters in this alphabet (I and J were not distinguished, nor were U and V; W and Y did not exist). Millions of texts were written, from great stone inscriptions to private letters scrawled on wax tablets, from elegant poems and histories carefully inked on papyrus scrolls to trade accounts scratched on broken pots. The tiny amount of texts that have survived are very precious because they contain information that ruined buildings and broken pots do not; writing is the only medium through which the Romans can still "speak" to us, about themselves and their world, about politics and what they thought and believed. But despite the importance of writing, most ordinary people were illiterate because of lack of education (p. 20) and because, in a world without printing, books had to be copied by hand, and so were rare and expensive.

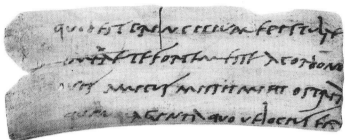

ROMAN HANDWRITING
Everyday handwriting was very different from the familiar capitals seen on inscriptions. This is a fragment of a letter in Latin, written in ink on a wooden tablet, preserved in a waterlogged pit at the fort of Vindolanda near Hadrian's Wall. Addressed to a decurion (like a corporal) named Lucius, it is about a welcome gift of oysters from a friend of the writer.

TRAJAN'S COLUMN
The inscription on the base of Trajan's Column in Rome is a famous example of beautifully proportioned Roman capitals which were painted on walls as well as carved in stone like these. This example has served as a model for Roman-style typefaces for several hundred years.

SOOTY INK
Fine soot was mixed with water and other ingredients to make ink, which was used for writing on papyrus, wood, or parchment.

ROMAN NUMERALS
Unlike the Arabic numbers we use today, Roman numerals were written as strings of symbols to be added together, with I for 1, V for 5, X for 10, C for 100, and so on. Large numbers were quite clumsy and complicated; for example, 1,778 in Roman numerals is MDCCLXXVIII. This made arithmetic very difficult.

The number four can be IV or IIII

WAXING LYRICAL
Beeswax was melted and poured into shallow cavities in wooden tablets to form a reusable writing surface.

Roman numerals are still used on some modern clocks and watches

Vellum

BLUE INKPOT
On the right is an inkpot from Egypt dating from the 1st century A.D. It is made of faience (a glassy material).

A PAIR OF WRITERS
These portraits from Pompeii show a woman with a wax tablet and stylus and a man with a papyrus scroll. The tablet has two leaves which folded together to protect the writing. Roman books consisted of one or more scrolls; books with pages were invented during late Roman times.

INLAID INKPOTS
Expensive inkpots to grace the desks of the wealthy were an opportunity for craftsworkers to display their skills (p. 42). On the left is a bronze example with elegant silver inlay and a lid to stop the ink from drying up. Below is a pair of bronze inkpots, covered with black niello (silver or copper sulfide) and inlaid with silver and gold depicting mythological scenes.

Spatula end for smoothing the wax to erase writing

Bronze stylus from Athens

Bronze pen

Iron stylus with bronze cover

Reed pen with split nib

Ivory stylus

HANGING INKPOT
Cords were once attached to the holes in this pottery inkpot and used for hanging or carrying.

PENS AND STYLI
Split-nib pens of reed and metal were used with ink to write on vellum, papyrus, or wood. The pointed stylus was designed for writing on wax tablets.

Papyrus

PAPYRUS AND VELLUM
Routine texts were written on reusable wax tablets or cheap thin leaves of wood. Egyptian papyrus (paper made from reed fibers) was used for more important documents like legal contracts. The finest books were written on vellum, sheets of wafer-thin animal skin (usually kid or lamb) which had a beautiful writing surface and great durability.

Craftsworkers and technology

ROMAN OBJECTS WHICH SURVIVE TODAY show that people were enormously skilled at working in all sorts of materials. Pottery was a large-scale industry in some areas, where wine jars (p. 60) and red Samian pots (p. 47) were made by the million in large workshops. Many of the potters were slaves or freedmen, and surviving names show that they, and other craftsworkers, were almost all men. Other crafts were on a much smaller scale, with individual artisans working from their own shops in towns like Pompeii. In those days skills were developed through trial and error to see what worked. Sons learned from their fathers, slaves from their masters or foremen; there were no college courses. Particularly talented craftsworkers, even if they were slaves, might hope to make their fortune with specially commissioned pieces for rich clients.

Face on flask

FACE FLASK
This mass-produced flask was probably used for holding a cosmetic. It was made by blowing a bubble of glass into a mold.

Teardrop-shaped decoration on beaker

MOLDED BEAKER
Mold blowing was the technique used to make this glass beaker. The mold had the teardrop decoration on the inside.

Glassworking

Glass had been made for centuries, but in the last century B.C. someone discovered that it was possible to blow glass into bubbles which could be formed quickly and cheaply into all kinds of useful vessels. Soon glass was being blown into molds, allowing mass production of bottles and highly decorated flasks. Glass was no longer a luxury, but became a widely used material. Sometimes broken glass was collected for recycling, as it is today.

BLUE RIBBED BOWL
Probably made by the older technique of pressing hot glass into a mold, this ribbed bowl is made of expensive blue glass. It may have been used as formal tableware at dinner parties (p. 46).

Glass jar

Bands of gold running through the glass

Lid of jar

PORTLAND VASE
A blown glass vessel, the Portland Vase is one of the most precious objects to survive from Roman times. A layer of white glass over the blue core was cut away with great skill to leave the elegant scenes of figures and foliage in white on a blue background. The task was probably performed by a jeweler, using the cameo technique developed to cut similar pictures from banded stone (p. 9). The procedure took many months. Such a famous work of art may well have belonged to the emperor – few others could have afforded it.

COLORFUL GLASS
Bands of colored glass and gold were incorporated into some vessels, like this delicate little jar and lid. It probably graced an elegant woman's dressing table (p. 18) and was used to store an expensive cosmetic.

Metalwork and jewelry

Gold, silver, lead, copper, iron, and other metals were widely used by the Romans. Mining, extracting metal from ore, and melting the metal to pour into molds were also understood. The Romans could not make furnaces hot enough to melt iron, so they forged it, hammering it into shape while it was hot. Metals were mixed to make alloys such as bronze, a mixture of copper and tin. Roman bronze often contained zinc as well, giving it a gold color.

SILVER MIRROR
Mirror glass had not yet been invented, so the Romans used polished metal instead. This polished silver mirror is attached to a separately made handle in the form of the club and lionskin of Hercules (the mythical Greek hero).

Outline of figure which was originally inlaid with gold foil

BRONZE PLAQUE
This small sheet of bronze bears a delicate gold foil inlay set into its surface. Outlines of figures were made before the inlaying took place.

SMITH'S TOOLS
The iron tongs were probably used by a smith to heat fairly small metal objects in a furnace.

Curved blade of knife

BONE-HANDLED KNIFE
Roman knives were often of this type, with a carved bone handle and a loop for hanging.

Loop for hanging knife up

JEWELER'S HOARD
These silver objects are part of a large hoard of jewelry, coins, and scrap silver that was buried at Snettisham, England, in the second century A.D. They represent the stock of materials and finished work of a silversmith.

Another tool of the trade, this iron file has lost its wooden handle

BITS AND PIECES
Fragments of old necklaces, bracelets, and rings were melted down to make new pieces.

Ingot of silver bullion

RINGS
There were 89 rings in the hoard, some with inset carved gems, Others shaped like snakes.

Boneworking

Bone was the plastic of the ancient world, used for making many everyday items such as knife handles, hairpins, and combs. It was also widely used for sword hilts. Fresh animal bone from the butcher's could be finely carved, and was also used for inlays on wooden boxes. Gaming counters and dice were frequently carved from bone (p. 38).

Woman's head on end of hairpin

BONE PINS
Large needles and pins were among the most common objects made from bone. These three are from Colchester, England. Hairpins were often necessary for the elaborate hairstyles worn by Roman women (p. 19).

BONE COMB
Most Roman combs were made like this one. The teeth were cut with a very fine saw.

Silver pendant for attaching to a necklace

This shaped stone found with the hoard is a polishing tool

First catch your dormouse

ROMAN COOKING SEEMS STRANGE to us today – for instance, one dish described by an ancient writer was dormice cooked in honey and poppyseed. The cooking also differed from ours because many of today's basic foods were not yet known. The Romans had no potatoes or tomatoes – these came from America. And pasta had not been invented. The Romans have a reputation for eating vast quantities of ornate and elaborate dishes, but in fact most ordinary people ate simple fare. Few of the poor had access to a kitchen, but bought hot food from the many bars, or *thermopolia*, in the streets of the towns. Their diet probably centered on bread, beans, lentils, and a little meat. Even well-off Romans, including emperors like Augustus, usually ate very little during the day. The only large meal was dinner (p. 46). Big houses had trained cooks who applied great artistry to complicated dishes. Disguising the food was fashionable, and this was done by adding sauces, herbs, and spices and by carving and serving it in novel ways. The look of food was as important as the taste.

Mice like these robbed many a Roman kitchen

UP-TO-DATE GRATER
The design of graters has changed little since Roman times. This modern-looking bronze grater was probably used for preparing cheese and vegetables.

COOK'S KNIFE
Serious cooks have always needed good sharp knives, especially to carve meat.

WOODEN SPOON
Wooden spoons would have been found in almost every Roman kitchen. Most wooden utensils have long since rotted away, but this example from Egypt is well preserved.

Lip in mortarium *for pouring out finished product*

MARKET FARE
This mosaic from Rome shows poultry, fish, and vegetables, probably freshly bought from the market stalls. Fresh fish was often very expensive, because of the difficulties of delivering it before it went rotten.

PESTLE AND MORTAR
The *mortarium*, or heavy grinding dish, was the Romans' equivalent to our modern electric food mixer. It was made of tough pottery with coarse grit in the surface, and was used with a pestle (seen inside the vessel) to grind foodstuffs into powders, pastes, or liquids. Using a *mortarium* was very hard work, and as the surface became worn, grit got into the food.

REUSABLE BOTTLE
Glass bottles with handles were used to trade valuable liquids, but when empty they were often used to store food in the kitchen, as we reuse glass jars today.

BRONZE SAUCEPAN
Bronze was widely used to make kitchen utensils because it could be precisely worked and it cooked the food evenly. But bronze is mostly copper, which can affect some foods and even make them poisonous. The pan on the left has been coated with silver to prevent this.

Saucepan was hung on kitchen wall by this hole

BRONZE STRAINER
Roman cooks used strainers as cooks do today: to drain boiled food and to separate juices and sauces. This one was made of bronze like the pan (left), and then an elegant pattern of holes was made afterward.

A ROMAN KITCHEN
A Pompeii kitchen scene shows an oven, with bronze pans still on top (p. 57). Roman ovens were fueled by wood or charcoal.

A BUN TIN?
We do not know exactly what this interesting utensil was used for. Perhaps it had a variety of uses, such as baking buns or poaching eggs.

Celery was a popular green vegetable in Rome

Thyme

Coriander seeds

Juniper berries

The Romans used a variety of herbs, easily grown in the warm Mediterranean climate, in their cooking

Pepper

Rue

Oregano

FISH SAUCE
A popular ingredient in Roman cookery was *garum*, a strong-tasting sauce made from fish, salt, and other ingredients. *Garum*, like olive oil and wine, was traded in *amphorae* (p. 60). The powerful flavor probably helped to disguise the taste of fish or meat, which was often not very fresh!

A Mediterranean fish such as this one would have been used in *garum*

A dinner party

AFTER A DAY'S WORK which started at dawn, and a visit to the baths (p. 38), the well-to-do Roman went home for the main meal of the day, dinner (*cena*). This normally started at two or three in the afternoon and was eaten at a leisurely pace over several hours. It was often more of a social event than just a meal, as there would frequently be guests, and entertainment between courses including clowns, dancers, or poetry readings, according to taste. People dressed for dinner in an elegant Greek robe called a *synthesis*, and ate reclining on large couches which held up to three people. Usually three couches were placed around the low dining table, to which servants brought the courses. The Romans did not use forks, so hands had to be frequently washed. Some dinner parties involved overeating, drunkenness, and revelling, but many were cultured occasions.

An 18th-century view of a Roman woman with grapes – perhaps a dancer at a dinner party

GLASS BOWL
The finest glassware adorned the tables of the rich. Besides being beautiful, glass was popular because it was easier to clean than most pottery (which was rarely glazed), and unlike bronze it did not taint certain foods (p. 45).

ROMAN WINE
Romans drank many varieties of wine, both dry and sweet. They were described as black, red, white, or yellow. Most wines had to be consumed within three or four years of production as they tended to go bad. Sometimes flavors were added, such as honey. Romans drank their wine mixed with water – to drink it neat was regarded as uncouth, although it was quite polite to belch. Some hosts served good wine to start with, but later substituted cheaper vintages, hoping everyone was too drunk to notice! Sadly, we will never know what Roman wines actually tasted like.

Roman wine was usually mixed with water, so was probably light in color

White swirling design in glass

Delicate patterns on side of cup

BRONZE JUG
Jugs for serving wine and water were made from pottery, glass, bronze, or silver, depending on how much the owner could afford.

A FEAST
This detail of a 19th-century painting by Edward A. Armitage gives some idea of the scene at an imperial banquet. The tables are laden with food and jugs of wine.

WINE CUPS
Decorated with graceful floral scrolls, birds, and insects, these beautiful silver cups originally had stems and feet. Pottery or glass wine cups would have been more commonly used.

Samian pottery

Glossy red pottery called Samian ware was very fashionable in the first and second centuries A.D. A range of shapes and sizes were made, mostly platters, bowls, and drinking cups, although exactly what people used each type for is not known. Made on a large scale at factories in Italy and Gaul, these vessels were shipped in millions all over the empire and beyond. They were elegant, quite easy to keep clean, and mostly designed to stack for easy transport and storage. A crate of Samian ware has been found at Pompeii (p. 57). It had just been delivered from Gaul and had not even been unpacked.

Samian platter with grapes

Samian wine jug

Samian cup

The Romans usually had fresh fruit for dessert, including figs

The dish is modern

Olives, widely grown in the Mediterranean regions, were probably eaten as appetizers, just as they are today

Asparagus tips for decoration

SONGBIRD SURPRISE
On the right is a recreation of an actual Roman dish from a surviving recipe. It consists of small songbirds served with an asparagus sauce and quail's eggs. The birds (in this case quails) would probably have been carefully arranged on a platter like this to delight and amaze the guests. There could not have been very much meat on such tiny birds, but this would have been one of many dishes, whose number and expense were a way a host might impress guests. The platter is modern.

Making music

THE ROMAN NOBILITY thought most music and musicians were rather vulgar, but music, song, and dance were popular with the people. Music was played in the theater and at private parties. It also accompanied religious ceremonies and other public events like gladiatorial shows. Many Roman instruments were of Greek origin, like the lyre (far right). Wind instruments were probably the most common types, from reed pipes to bronze horns. These produced loud notes suitable for outdoor events. The most complicated instrument used was the water organ, invented by a Greek in the 3rd century B.C. The water organ used a pump to force water into a closed chamber, thus compressing the air inside. A system of hand-operated valves then released bursts of this compressed air into a set of musical pipes, producing notes or chords like a modern organ. Unfortunately, even though we know so much about Roman music and what people thought about it, we will never know what it actually sounded like.

PAN WITH PIPES
The bronze statuette above shows the rural god Pan (p. 51) with the traditional shepherd's instrument still called pan-pipes. They consist of a row of cane whistles of different lengths which produce different notes.

MUSIC AND DANCE
The detail from a mosaic on the left shows a woman with castanets dancing to the music of a man playing double pipes. Bands of such performers played in the street or were hired to appear at dinner parties.

DOUBLE TROUBLE
A bronze satyr (woodland god) plays the double pipes, a pair of simple flutes. There is no modern instrument like them. They must have been very difficult to learn to play – both flutes had to be blown at the same time.

FRENZIED DANCE
Music and dance were important parts of worship in some cults and could help worshipers achieve a state of ecstasy. The dancers seen on the stone relief above are probably followers of the goddess Isis (p. 50). They are working themselves into a state of frenzied joy or mystical trance by rhythmic movements.

RODENT RHYTHM
A caricature of a simple straight bronze horn is seen in this comic figurine of a musical rat or mouse.

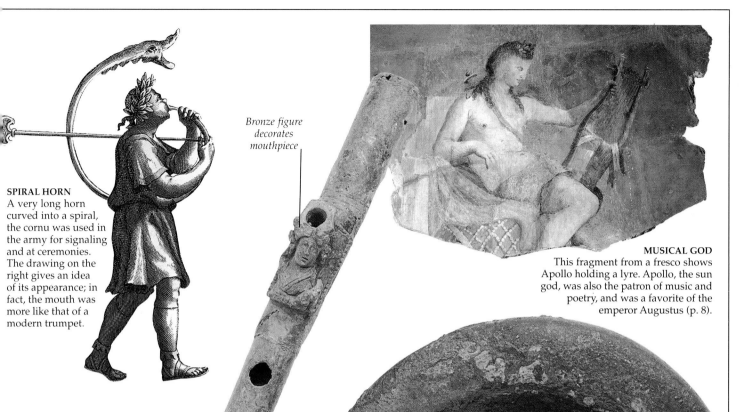

SPIRAL HORN
A very long horn curved into a spiral, the cornu was used in the army for signaling and at ceremonies. The drawing on the right gives an idea of its appearance; in fact, the mouth was more like that of a modern trumpet.

Bronze figure decorates mouthpiece

MUSICAL GOD
This fragment from a fresco shows Apollo holding a lyre. Apollo, the sun god, was also the patron of music and poetry, and was a favorite of the emperor Augustus (p. 8).

FLUTE
Like a modern flute, this Roman example was played by blowing across a hole. It has been restored from corroded fragments, probably incorrectly, and cannot now be played.

Finger holes, covered to achieve different notes

BRONZE CYMBALS
Found at Praeneste in Italy, these bronze cymbals have holes where there were once leather or cord straps for holding them. The Romans played only a limited range of percussion instruments, which included the sistrum (a metal rattle mainly used for religious purposes) and simple tambourine-like drums.

A world of many gods

ACROSS THE ROMAN EMPIRE people worshiped hundreds of different gods and goddesses, demigods (half gods), and spirits. These were depicted as large human forms, like the Greek gods. Everyone was expected to offer sacrifices to the important gods of the Roman state such as Jupiter, and to the guardian spirit of the emperor. Many worshiped at their local deity, or chose foreign gods who offered comfort and hope for the afterlife – for example Mithras or Isis. There were gods to protect the house (p. 23), gods of healing, in fact gods of all aspects of life. Generally people tolerated the beliefs of others. However, the Christians were an important exception. Their beliefs prevented them from sacrificing to the Roman gods, and so they were thought to be dangerous unbelievers who imperiled Rome by offending the gods. As a result, the Christians were persecuted from time to time by the Romans (p. 32).

GOD OF THUNDER
The king of the Roman gods was Jupiter, known as Best and Greatest, a sky god whose symbols were the eagle and the thunderbolt. Jupiter was a lot like the Greek god Zeus. His main home was the great temple on the Capitoline Hill in Rome.

WOMEN'S GODDESS
Juno, the wife of Jupiter, was the patron goddess of women. The clay figurine above shows her enthroned with a peacock, her symbol.

TEMPLE OF AUGUSTUS AND LIVIA
Most emperors were declared gods after their deaths, and temples were built at which to worship them. Augustus and his wife, Livia (p. 9) were both made into gods. The well-preserved temple which still stands in Vienne, France, was built in their honor. Many Roman temples looked like this. Each temple was thought of as the home of the god or goddess it was dedicated to. Offerings were made at an altar in front of the building (p. 52).

EGYPTIAN GODS
Some Romans worshiped mysterious foreign gods, as well as their own traditional ones. The Egyptian goddess Isis (left) was one of the most popular of these, and was worshiped with the god Serapis (above). The religion was about the cycle of life, death, and rebirth, and its secret ceremonies gave worshipers a sense of belonging and hope for the next world.

WISE GODDESS
Warlike Minerva, with her helmet and armor, was very much like the famous Greek goddess Athena. Minerva was the goddess of handicrafts and wisdom. She is often depicted on soldiers' armor.

MARS AND VENUS

Mars, the god of war, is still remembered in the name of the month March. Gauls and Britons came to worship many of their own gods as versions of similar Roman ones, usually Mars or Mercury, the messenger of the gods (p. 53). The silver plaque from Britain on the right is dedicated to a Romano-British "mixed" god called Mars Alator. Venus, the Roman goddess of love, beauty, and fertility, was said to be the divine ancestor of the family of Julius Caesar.

Gilded silver plaque was a temple offering

Inscription says that the plaque was given to fulfill a promise to the god

Julius Caesar built a temple to Venus in Rome

GOD OF LIGHT

Mithraism was a Persian cult concerned with the eternal struggle of good and evil. Mithras was worshiped by many soldiers – it was a "men only" religion. The statue shows Mithras slaying the bull whose blood gave life to the universe.

A RIOTOUS GOD

Also called Dionysus, Bacchus was a Greek god who promised rebirth to his followers. He was also the god of wine, so not surprisingly his festivals could be riotous! Theater started as part of his worship.

Bacchus holds bunches of grapes as a symbol of wine

THE CULT OF CYBELE

Cybele was a mother goddess from Turkey. Her religion was about fertility and the cycle of death and rebirth. It was a very emotional religion, and sometimes her priests would work themselves into a frenzy and castrate themselves for her. These bronze clamps may have been used for this gruesome ritual.

Busts of the gods decorate the clamps

The monster is eating a man

GOAT GOD

One of many Greek gods adopted by Rome, Pan was a son of Hermes (Mercury). Half man, half goat, he was a god of mountains and lonely places, of flocks and shepherds, and he played panpipes (p. 48). He could cause herds of animals to "panic" and stampede.

CELTIC GOD

The Britons and Gauls believed in some grim gods, like this monster, and sacrificed people to them.

Worship and sacrifice

PEOPLE FEARED THE GODS and sought to win their favor or ask for their help. People would pray and make offerings at temples to seek divine favors or to give thanks afterward. Offerings came in all shapes and sizes, from coins and brooches left by the poor, to silver statues donated by the rich. Augustus promised Mars a new temple if the god helped him to avenge the death of Caesar, and today the remains of the Temple of Mars the Avenger can still be seen in Rome. People also sacrificed food and drink, and burned incense on altars. Animal sacrifices were common, ranging from a single bird to a whole herd of cattle. There were few full-time priests or priestesses, except for the Vestal Virgins, who guarded the holy flame of the goddess Vesta in Rome. Most priests were important people in public life for whom a priesthood was one of many duties. The emperor was chief priest of Rome. The title was Pontifex Maximus, or chief bridge builder, because he bridged the space between the people and the gods.

PRIESTESS SACRIFICING
A priestess pours a libation (probably milk, oil, or wine) onto an altar as an offering to a goddess or god. In a number of religions women were the only or the main worshipers. The cults of Vesta, Isis, and Cybele were particularly associated with women.

LIBATION JUG
A bronze jug such as this was used for holding liquids to pour during sacrifices. The jug, bowl, and knife are often shown in religious scenes with other priestly gear.

Lion-headed handle

UNDER THE KNIFE
Animals were sacrificed in various ways; larger beasts like cattle were felled with an axe. Then a knife was used to slit the animal's throat and cut it open. Its inner organs were removed for the priests to study (see opposite page).

LIBATION BOWL
A libation bowl was used to pour liquids into the fire on top of the altar. The smoke from this and from the burned flesh would ascend to the heavens to please the god.

CURSE TABLET
One way to seek revenge on enemies was to place a curse on them at the local temple. This lead plaque from the temple at Uley in Gloucestershire, England, asks Mercury to make the thieves who stole a valuable animal fall sick until they return it.

THE BARE BONES
Certain animals were chosen to be sacrificed to certain gods. Mercury's "holy animals" were the cock and the ram, and the many thousands of bones found at Uley show that people sacrificed sheep and chickens in his honor there. Above are some of the chicken bones.

OFFERING A SACRIFICE
On this relief from Italy a silenus, or Greek woodland spirit, is shown making an offering at an altar. Sileni were companions of the god Bacchus (Dionysus, p. 51). You can see the fire on the altar and the libation being poured.

DIVINE MESSENGER
Above is a little bronze statue of Mercury, messenger of the gods, which was left as an offering at his temple at Uley. Perhaps it was a thank-you offering for a favor granted, or a gift and a reminder of a request not yet fulfilled.

LIVER IN THE HAND
A fragment of a marble statue shows a hand holding an animal's liver. A special priest with the Etruscan title *haruspex* would read the god's will from the liver's shape and condition. It was thought to be a bad sign if the organ was deformed in any way.

SACRIFICIAL ALTAR
Roman altars stood in the open, outside the front of the temple. The cult figure of the god was kept inside.

The way that the sacred chickens ate showed whether or not the gods approved of a plan

BOAR TO THE SLAUGHTER
An attendant leads a boar to the altar for sacrifice. Its inner organs would be burned on the altar as offerings to the gods, while the good meat was cooked for the faithful in a sacrificial meal. Roman religion could be very practical!

Healing the sick

MEDICAL SCIENCE was still in its infancy during Roman times, and causes of disease were not well understood. Most Romans believed that illness could be caused by witchcraft, curses, and the gods. Many sought supernatural cures for their ailments and traveled to distant healing shrines or spas such as Bath, England (p. 38). Doctors, almost all men and mainly Greek, were expensive and some were frauds. Even skilled physicians could not save people from afflictions which today can be cured by a dose of antibiotics or a few days in the hospital. Appendicitis, for example, today remedied by a routine operation, was always fatal. Romans had some effective drugs, but with no real anesthetics, surgery was terrifying, agonizing, and dangerous. Despite the efforts of the best doctors, it is not surprising that people sought miracle cures from the gods!

SIGNET RINGS
The rings above depict Asklepios (see opposite) and Hygeia, an angel-like figure symbolizing health. The rings were probably worn to ward off illness.

VOTIVE EAR
When visiting a temple to ask the god for a cure, people often left votive offerings of the afflicted part (in this case a model of the right ear) to remind the god of the requested cure.

VOTIVE LEG
The bronze model leg above was dedicated to a god by a man named Caledus, probably in gratitude for a cured leg injury or infection.

PHYSICIAN AND CHILD
This marble tombstone (left) shows a Greek doctor examining a child. On the ground can be seen an outsize "cupping vessel" used for extracting blood and, it was believed, the "vicious humor" which caused the disease.

Elecampane was used to help the digestion

HEALING HERBS
Many plant materials were known to have medicinal properties and were used to make drugs and ointments.

Fenugreek was used for treating pneumonia

Sage, a powerful healer, was sacred to the Romans

Fennel was thought to have calming properties

Rosemary was widely used in Roman medicine

The Roman writer Pliny listed 40 remedies with mustard as the main ingredient

Roman soldiers were fed a daily ration of garlic for health

INSULA TIBERINA
After a plague in the 3rd century B.C., a temple to Aesculapius (the Greek Asklepios), god of healing, was established at Rome. It was sited on this small island in the Tiber River, which remained a center of healing right into medieval times.

The saw has lost its handle

MEDICAL INSTRUMENTS
On this page is a range of surgical and other instruments used by Roman doctors, mostly made in durable, well-finished bronze. Sets of doctor's equipment have been found in graves.

A spoon for giving liquid medicine

Decorative handle of probe

SAW AND FORCEPS
The very fine toothed saw above was used for cutting bone during amputations. Tweezer-like forceps (left) were used to extract splinters or fragments of tissue.

Scalpel (the iron blade has rusted away)

End of bronze catheter

Folding knife

PROBE
Before operations probes like the one on the left were used to explore the wound.

THIS IS GOING TO HURT...
The Roman wall-painting on the right shows the legendary hero Aeneas having an arrow-head removed from his thigh with pincer-like forceps. The Roman army had doctors skilled in the treatment of such wounds.

SPECULUM
This device was used by doctors for internal examinations.

Handle of speculum

HOOKS
Above is a double-ended traction hook for holding sinews and blood vessels out of the way during operations. On the left is a smaller hook to hold the incision open.

Central pivot

CATHETER
Fine bronze curved tubes like this were used for draining the bladder of patients who had difficulty passing urine.

Squeezing the handles together (above) opened these prongs

Spatula for mixing and applying ointments

Death and burial

THE ROMANS LIVED CLOSER TO DEATH than we do today – their life expectancy was generally short, and disease was common. This was because of a combination of poor diet, lack of medical care, and hard living conditions. Children were particularly at risk, with perhaps one in three dying in infancy. There were many hazards even for adults; women were especially vulnerable to the risks of childbirth. It is unlikely that more than half of the population survived to be fifty, although a few lived to their eighties and beyond. Not surprisingly, death was commonplace in Roman communities, and there were many rites surrounding it. Funeral fashions changed. Cremation (burning) was preferred at first, then inhumation (burying the body intact). Today study of these burials and the remains of the people themselves can reveal many details about them.

IN THE CATACOMBS
In Rome, Christians buried their dead in catacombs – a series of underground tunnels and chambers with niches in the walls for coffins. The underground chapels were there for holding funeral services rather than hiding from persecution (p. 51); the catacombs were not secret.

MARBLE URN
The ashes of the cremated dead were put in containers and deposited in family tombs or in larger cemeteries. The inscription on this beautifully carved marble burial urn tells that it contains the remains of a woman named Bovia Procula, a "most unfortunate mother." Perhaps she died in childbirth. The ivy leaves carved on it were sacred to Bacchus, and probably symbolize hope of rebirth.

REMEMBERING AVITA
Many Roman tombstones echo their sadness across the centuries. The tombstone above is that of a ten-year-old girl named Avita, shown as her parents wanted to remember her, with her books and her pet dog.

ACROSS THE RIVER STYX
A child lies on her deathbed, surrounded by her grieving parents and other mourners. The Romans followed the Greek belief that the dead were ferried across the river Styx to Hades (the Underworld), and so they often put a coin in the mouth of the body with which the soul could pay the ferryman. The funeral would consist of a solemn procession to the cemetery, or to the place of cremation. After burning, the ashes were collected and put into an urn (below).

STREET OF TOMBS
Roman religious law forbade burials within towns, a rule which also reduced the risk of disease. Cemeteries grew up outside the gates. The best spots were next to the road, where passersby would see the graves and remember the people buried there, so giving them a kind of immortality. Remembering the dead, especially the family ancestors, was very important to the Romans.

Buried under ash

Perhaps the most famous "burial" of all was the burial of towns around the base of Mount Vesuvius, Italy, in A.D. 79. This volcano exploded with violent intensity one summer afternoon and cast a rain of burning pumice and ashes all over the towns and countryside around it, burying everything up to 13 ft (4 m) deep. Pompeii is the most famous of these buried cities, frozen in time by the deep blanket of pumice and dust. Life ended so suddenly in Pompeii that we are able to learn a lot about the lives of the people there, and many bodies of people who failed to leave in time have been found. It is not just the bones which survive. The ashes hardened around the bodies, so that although the flesh has long since gone, hollow "molds" of their original shapes are still to be found.

GLASS URN
The ashes of the dead were also put into pots and glass vessels like this urn. There is no inscription giving the name of the dead person, but the fragments of bone might be enough to indicate if it was a man or a woman.

VICTIM OF VESUVIUS
Above is the plaster cast of the "mold" of the body of a man caught in Pompeii by the eruption. Often the shape of clothes and shoes can be made out. The shapes of animals, including a dog, have been preserved in the same way. These figures speak for themselves of the horror experienced by people frozen in struggling poses or desperately trying to shield themselves from the ashes and fumes.

Fragments of burnt bone from the urn

PLOWING THE LAND
The bronze model above shows a British plowman at work with his team of cattle, preparing the ground for sowing grain. He is bundled up and hooded against the cold.

Country life

ALTHOUGH ROMAN LIFE WAS CENTERED IN CITIES, most people lived in the countryside, working the land, growing crops, tending vines and flocks, or managing olive groves and woodlands. The farm workers produced the food, materials, and fuel on which the splendid cities depended. It was a backbreaking life of endless toil for men, women, and children, many of whom were slaves. Much of Italy was divided into huge estates owned by very rich people whose main interests were in town but whose wealth mostly came from their farmlands. The rich liked to escape the heat of town in the summer and retreat to their estates, where they could enjoy the countryside. They built themselves fine houses (villas) on their estates or by the sea, with all the luxuries, such as baths (p. 38).

REAPING HOOK
Sickles like this were used for cutting grain. Bending down all day to use such a short-handled tool must have caused back pain.

EMMER WHEAT
A range of cereals was grown in Roman times, including emmer, an ancient variety of wheat, seen here both as ripened ears and as threshed grain ready to make into bread and other foods. Emmer is very nutritious, with twice as much protein as modern bread wheats. Bringing the grain in from the fields and threshing, winnowing, and storing it were jobs as toilsome as cutting it.

BOAR HUNT
Animals were hunted both on foot and on horseback, the hunters armed with spears and accompanied by dogs to find and flush out the prey. Hunting could be very dangerous, as this mosaic from Sicily shows.

THE THRILL OF THE CHASE
Roman huntsmen enjoyed the thrill of chasing the wild boar with its great speed and razor-sharp tusks. Its ferocity is well captured in the bronze statuette above.

This finely preserved wall painting is from the villa of the empress Livia (p. 9). It reveals the elegance and magnificence of the very richest Roman country houses, with imposing and shady colonnaded corridors, gardens, and pools.

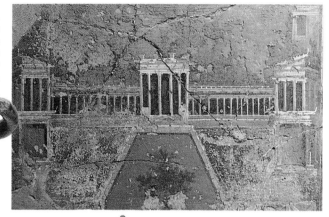

BRONZE BULL

Keeping livestock for food, dairy products, and leather was a major part of Roman farming. Some areas of Italy were turned into huge slave-run cattle ranches, where bulls like this splendid beast were kept for breeding.

SHEEP SHEARS

Iron shears like these have been used for sheep shearing and cloth manufacture ever since Roman times.

Winemaking

Cultivating grape vines and olive trees was (and still is) very important in sunny Mediterranean lands like Italy. Olives and grapes were of course eaten, but the olive oil and grape juice were perhaps more important. Fermenting alcohol from grape juice to make wine was already an ancient art in Roman times, and in a world without coffee or tea, wine was even more widely consumed than it is today (p. 46).

Above, a modern drawing of a Roman relief shows cupids picking grapes, stomping them, and (left) sacrificing to the gods

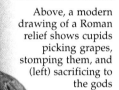

Glass "grape" flask

SHEPHERD BOY

The wealthy Roman who owned this lovely silver figurine of a shepherd boy must have had a very romantic view of country life – a far cry from the hard reality.

Lamb peeping out of shepherd's shoulder bag

NILE LANDSCAPE
A mosaic from Pompeii depicts the wildlife of the Nile River in Egypt. Fishing and catching fowl were a way of life for many. The Romans often exploited the natural resources of the lands they ruled.

BRONZE GOAT
Goats were kept by farmers for milk, cheese, and meat.

Transportation, travel, and trade

PERHAPS THE GREATEST GIFT Rome gave the ancient world was the Roman Peace. For the only time in history until then, the entire Mediterranean and the lands around were at peace and under one government. The Roman navy suppressed pirates, and the army laid the famous network of great highways. These roads were built with military needs in mind, but they helped to open up the empire and, with the open seaways, helped to tie the many peoples and provinces together. Trade and prosperity grew. Merchant ships carried the wines of Italy and Spain to Gaul and Britain, while huge freighters, the supertankers of their day, bore the grain harvest of North Africa to feed the people of the city of Rome. Wild animals for the amphitheater were collected from many countries (p. 32). Soldiers, politicians, traders, and even some tourists traveled across the empire, and with them came new fashions and ideas. For instance, the Roman Peace helped Christianity to spread from its Eastern homeland, along the roads and seaways, to the cities of the West.

DONKEY AND PANNIERS
Animals were used to transport goods. They pulled wagons and carried loads in baskets called panniers. This bronze statuette shows that Roman donkeys were as stubborn as modern ones!

STORAGE VESSELS
These pottery jars, called *amphorae*, held Italian wine, mostly for selling to other countries. Their shape allowed them to be tightly packed together in the holds of merchant ships. Other shapes of amphora were used to carry olive oil or fish sauce for cooking (p. 44).

Dupondius, worth two asses

As

Aureus, worth 100 asses

Sestertius, worth four asses

Denarius, worth 16 asses

READY MONEY
Coins were minted by the emperor mainly to pay the soldiers and to collect taxes. Almost everyone across the empire used this common money, which made trading simpler. Well-preserved silver *denarii* can be found today as far away as India.

A MERCHANT SHIP
A stone relief from Carthage shows a small ship and its helmsman. In the summer months laden freighters sailed the seas as far as Britain and India. Lacking compasses they hugged the coast, but feared to get too close in case the wind wrecked them on the shore. Sailing was dangerous and usually ceased during the winter.

This weight allowed the balance to work like a steelyard

BRONZE SCALES
There were two common types of scales which Roman traders used for weighing everything from vegetables to gold: simple bronze balances like this, and another type called a steelyard (below). Both kinds are still used in many countries.

A steelyard for weighing the meat

The chains are modern replacements

AT THE BUTCHER'S
A stone relief shows a butcher at work with a cleaver. Joints of meat hang from the rail above. The seated woman is probably a customer, holding a shopping list on her lap and waiting for her order.

The pans could be lifted off the hooks and bags used instead

Hook for weighing bags

BRONZE STEELYARD
The steelyard was hung up by the upper hook. The item to be weighed was attached to the lower hook on the left, and the weight on the right was moved along until the arm balanced horizontally. The weight could then be read off from a scale inscribed along the arm.

The weight is shaped like an acorn

OFFICIAL WEIGHT
This bronze weight from Turkey is decorated with a bust of Hercules. It bears the names of two local officials. Weights were checked by officials to keep traders from cheating with false measures.

The twilight of Rome

GREAT CHANGES OVERCAME the Roman Empire after A.D. 200. There were constant clashes with the "barbarians" to the north and the warlike Persians in the east. There was eco-nomic chaos, and frequent civil wars as generals once more struggled for power. Eventually Diocletian and his three co-emperors managed to restore peace, but at a price; the empire groaned under the weight of a growing and corrupt administrative system and an increasingly powerless army. One of Diocletian's successors, Constantine, believed that he came to power with the help of the Christian god, and by his death in A.D. 337 Christianity had not only emerged from the shadows but had become the state religion. By A.D. 400, paganism was declining and being repressed. In A.D. 395 the empire was finally divided into two states, east and west. They were to have very different fates.

A CHRISTIAN FAMILY
This fragment of gold glass depicts a family with the early Christian *chi* (X)-*rho* (P) symbol (made from the first two letters of Christ's name in Greek).

THE LATIN WEST...
Below is a silver statuette representing Rome, the old, pagan, western capital. Both figures come from the 4th-century Esquiline treasure found in Rome.

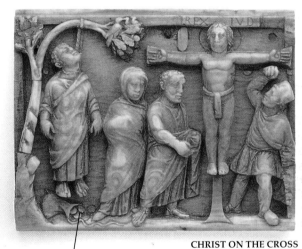

The 30 pieces of silver paid to Judas for his betrayal

CHRIST ON THE CROSS
A detailed design on an ivory box depicts the crucifixion of Christ and, on the left, Judas hanging himself. It dates from about A.D. 420. Christ was often shown without a beard in Roman times.

Below is a fanciful view of the baptism of Constantine, the first Christian emperor

...AND THE GREEK EAST
Above is a personification of Constantinople, the new eastern capital and Christian city founded by Constantine. Today it is called Istanbul.

The decline of the West

As Christianity triumphed, the western empire was beginning to break up under the strain of military defeat and economic crisis. The Rhine frontier was overrun in A.D. 406, and the German peoples poured into the empire. In A.D. 410 Rome itself was sacked, and in A.D. 476 the last western emperor lost his power. Rome itself had fallen, but the eastern empire lived on.

RADIATE BROOCHES
The Germans were not all the rough warriors the Romans thought them to be. Some were skilled craftsworkers and made spectacular jewelry. The brooches on the left, for example, were made by the Ostrogoths in about A.D. 500 from silver, gold, green glass, and red garnet.

Iron spearhead

Red garnet inlaid in the gold

Two iron arrowheads

WEAPONS OF WAR
These arms, an iron spearhead and two arrowheads, come from the grave of one of the Frankish conquerors of Gaul. By the time these weapons were buried, during the 6th century, the new Frankish kingdom had been established. During these centuries the barbarians were also gradually converted to Christianity.

The barbarians
Rome feared the Germans and other "barbarian" peoples to the north, who were becoming very powerful in the 4th century. When the barbarians finally burst into the western empire they settled in the newly conquered lands and founded many of the states of modern Europe; the Franks turned Gaul into France, and the Angles and Saxons turned Roman Britain into Saxon England.

ATTILA AND THE POPE
The Huns from central Asia were the most feared invaders of all, and they devastated 5th-century Europe. This medieval drawing shows the Pope negotiating with their leader Attila in A.D. 452. It was believed that this saved the city of Rome from further destruction.

The East survives
The heavily populated and wealthy East also experienced wars, but it survived, more and more precariously, until 1453. It still called itself "Roman," but this Greek-speaking Christian state was very different from old Rome, and is today referred to as the Byzantine Empire.

Artemis, the Greek goddess of hunting

BYZANTINE EMPEROR
The bronze steelyard weight (p. 61) on the right depicts a 7th-century emperor. He looks more like a medieval king than a Roman emperor, and the style of art is also very different from earlier times; Byzantium was a medieval state.

MEDALLION
The Christian Byzantines preserved the heritage of their Greek and Roman ancestors in their libraries and treasuries, and their artists still sometimes used pagan images, such as the figure on this sixth-century gold medallion. The classical heritage was rediscovered by the West at the end of the Middle Ages.

Index

Acknowledgments

Dorling Kindersley would like to thank:
The Department of Greek and Roman Antiquities, The British Museum, for providing ancient artifacts for photography.
Emma Cox for her invaluable assistance in making ancient artifacts available for photography.
Celia Clear, British Museum Publications.
Mr. B. Cook and Mr. D. Bailey, The Department of Greek and Roman Antiquities.
Dr. T.W. Potter and Miss C. Johns, The Department of Prehistoric and Romano-British Antiquities.
Mr. D. Kidd and Mr. D. Buckton, The Department of Medieval and Later Antiquities.

Peter Connolly for his superb model of the Colosseum on pp. 28-29, and Brian Lancaster for his assistance.
Thomas Keenes for his work on the initial stages of the book.
Louise Pritchard for editorial assistance.
Jane Coney for her design assistance, and providing of props.
Lester Cheeseman for his desktop publishing expertise.
Ermine Street Guard; pp. 10-11.
Jane Parker for the index.

Picture credits

t=top b=bottom l=left r=right
c=center

Aerofilms: 26bc
Aldus Archive/Syndication International: 23cl; /Museo Nazionale, Naples 59bl
Alinari: /Museo Nazionale, Naples 55bc
Ancient Art & Architecture Collection: 38bl, 40c
Bridgeman Art Library: /Musee Crozatier, Le Puy en Velay 12cl; /Antiken Museum, Staatliches Museen, W. Berlin 22cr, 25br, 32cl, 39tl, 46bl
British Film Institute: 33br
British Museum: 12br, 19tl, 19bl, 22tl, 23bl, 42bl, 51bl, 56bl, 57tl, 59c
J. Allan Cash Photolibrary: 17cl
Michael Dixon, Photo Resources: 19br, 20tl, 35bl, 34tr
Mary Evans Picture Library: 7br, 8cl, 14tl, 16bl, 18cr, 25c, 30tl, 56tr, 62bc, 63tr

Werner Forman Archive: 48bl, 49tr, 53tr, 57br
Sonia Halliday Photographs: 32tl, 58cr
Robert Harding Picture Library: 37tl, 59tr, 61tr
Simon James: 12 br, 14cr, 24cl, 26 tl, 27 cl, 27 cr, 28bl, 35tl, 37tc, 38tl, 44c, 45tr, 50cr, 57c
Kobal Collection: 34cl
Louvre/© Reunion des Musees Nationaux: 20-21b
Mansell Collection: 7t, 13tl
Scala: 25bl; /Citta del Vaticano, Rome 13tr, 48cl; /Museo della Terme, Rome 18bl; /Musei Capitolini, Rome 36tl; /Museo Nazionale, Naples 36br, 41tl; /Museo Civico, Albenga 60cl

Illustrations by: Peter Bull, p. 27; p. 38, Eugene Fleury, p. 7

Picture Reasearch: Kathy Lockley